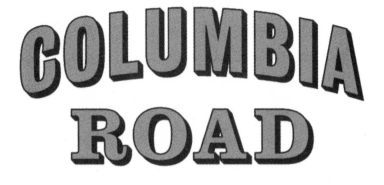

COLUMBIA ROAD

Of Blood and Belonging

Linda Wilkinson

For Bella and Harry

Mum and Nan, *c.* 1932

Clara and Alice

Me (*right*) outside the Garcias and Daltrey's,
Columbia Road, 1955

Mum   Clara   Diamond Lil   Nan   Alice
VE Day celebration, 8 May 1945

Prologue

Memoirs, like plays, have a through line. They can be linear, or non-linear. Run from birth to death, or describe a brief three weeks that change a life. There is no one format, no one way, except that the work is your recollection of your truth.

I never really left Bethnal Green. I carried it inside of me. Even when I thought I'd moved on to other spheres or inhabited different worlds it was there, even if I wasn't always aware of it.

Returning to Columbia Road after an absence of many years unleashed what can only be described as a tidal wave of emotions and recollections, and it is of no great surprise that I have spent the twenty-odd years since I became an author writing about the history of the place.

Coming home need not have been inevitable. I could have continued my life elsewhere, but I know now that there would always have been a part of me that was absent, empty of a richness that back then I barely understood.

Chapter 1

The Return

I come from a family of storytellers and mythmakers; the sorters of reality who keep tales of the ordinary alive. Yarns that may be true, or have the merest soupçon of truth embedded within them. Stories that give a relish to the belonging that we feel towards a person or a place.

I haven't thought about this for years, yet as I sit next to the Man with a Van as we crawl towards the Old Street roundabout I find myself remembering. It seems the best way to blot out both the mindless chatter emanating from the driver's mouth and the radio which is set to full blast. In the back of the beaten-up vehicle is the furniture I have culled from the past few years of my life and with which I am now heading home.

I am not drowning in sentimentality about this. I know where I am going has little beauty. No landscape to take the breath away, no cultural highlights of note, just a street of Victorian shops and houses to which I now know I undoubtedly belong.

It is Friday, 16 May 1986, and the sun is shining as the van pulls up outside the house that Carol and I now own. It is quiet, so quiet, more so than I recall it being. Carol has beaten me here, the street door is open and she is unloading the final parts of her life from her old Datsun.

The Man with a Van luckily wants to return to north London, to climb up the A1000 towards the cheaper end of East Finchley from whence he came, so there is no delay in his desire to empty his vehicle and be gone. I give him a minor tip and he goes off in a belch of fumes and black smoke.

The sky is blue and small, intensely white, cotton ball clouds drift across it. Before I close the door I glance to my right. Less than twenty yards away I can see the sign with the name of the next street. An old sign proclaiming 'Columbia Road'. I have, it has to be said, been less than truthful about my desire to return to my roots, having pushed the economic argument with Carol that we could afford a house here for what a flat would cost anywhere else. That much is true. The deceit I have peddled has been that nobody would remember me. Convincing her that our sexuality would be no problem to East Enders had fallen flat, so I had lied to close the deal. It never works.

Within five minutes of my arrival the doorbell rang and my cover is blown.

Carol is almost quaking with fear as she finds me in the garden, having just suffered her first onslaught of an East End stare followed by the demand of, 'Where is she?'

'Somebody wants you,' she says, bewildered, as I head towards the open door.

She is older and her hair is no longer pure ginger, but shot through with white. Her teeth, long gone, are replaced by badly fitting dentures which she rattles around inside her mouth like some out of kilter washing machine. We had never been friends, her gossipy nature and the difference in age had set us far apart, but there she is, one of the constants. She crosses her arms across now flaccid breasts. She is Ginger Lil.

'You're back then,' she says with a mixture of curiosity and self-satisfaction.

'I am,' I say, and smile.

Lil stands on slippered tiptoe in a mock attempt at looking over my shoulder towards where she thinks Carol hides.

'She your friend?' The 'friend' is accented, weighted, full of Lil's unsophisticated attempt at hidden meaning, yet also laced with humour.

I nod.

'I had a "friend" like that during the war. She upped and died on me. Hope you have better luck.'

And she is gone, walking towards Columbia Road. At the corner of Baxendale Street, a mere ten yards away, she stops, turns and grins toothlessly, her dentures by now residing in a pocket. The wave and wink are warm, and I return the greeting with a laugh.

* * *

Lil had been there when I was born, well, not technically there. Mother had gone into labour during a snowy cold snap and Lil had helped her walk up to the hospital. There was no thought of a taxi, bus or ambulance in weather

3

like that and, as my mum was too old for home delivery, she'd had to get there somehow, trailing her broken waters behind her.

It was 13 March 1952 and Mum was thirty-five years old. In those days anything over thirty was perceived as an ancient age to be producing a child. So acutely did she feel this shame that she had taken pills to try and prevent my arrival into the world. It was a secret that she had never shared with anyone else, and people look at me in horror when I voice it. She had described to me how distressed she had been when the early menopause she thought she was having turned out to be me. The repugnance with which her swelling figure was viewed had upset her profoundly. It was as if the sexual act was restricted only to the young, without any quarter given to the fact that her husband had been overseas during much of the war years thus interrupting her fecundity. What few knew was that during the late 1940s she had suffered a septic miscarriage of twins and had been told that she was probably infertile. In 1952, as she lay expecting the impending delivery of this late child, the irony of her pariah status was profound.

She was a beauty, my mum, and to outsiders seemed to glide through life. Unlike many she had not been forced to take up relations with other men in order to survive those years of privation. She had not had to rely on the kindness of servicemen from more affluent nations to feed her family. She saw no stain on the women who had been forced into this, nor did she regard the frequent offspring of those liaisons with any disdain. It had just been a fact of war.

During those years, her life had been 'blessed', as she so frequently put it, by the presence of the Garcias. Jews of Spanish extraction who ran the grocer's shop opposite our house in Columbia Road.

'If it hadn't been for Jack and his wife, I don't know what would have happened,' she said to me during one of our pre-bedtime chats.

'I was really up against it.'

Such glorious moments they were, these shared conversations of my youth. Mum in a quilted dressing gown and smelling of talcum powder, me on her lap groggy with the lateness of the hour and the warm milk we drank at bedtime.

Every single day of my childhood we would cross the road and buy something from the Garcias' shop. A sliver of cheese, a cut of freshly boiled ham, just something.

The hand-cranked machine and the elegant, balletic way that Jack caught the slices of meat before laying them reverently onto shiny greaseproof paper are indented in my memory. The smell, the sounds and in the background Mum saying, 'Jack, I can pay you back now,' and he waving her into silence with his hand.

Coins would be passed across the counter, the till would ting and we would go home with the small, beautifully wrapped parcels which formed the substance of the lunches she made for Dad.

'He won't take any money,' she would say and Dad would shrug.

'But Harry, without him we would have starved.'

'They are good people Bella, don't insult him by labouring the point.'

'It doesn't seem right.'

'One day he'll need our help and we shan't be afraid to give it.'

Mollified she would go about making the sandwiches.

In the early hours of 14 March, Mother entered the final stage of labour, a fact which was ignored by the nursing staff, she being old and having no right to be there. They left her alone while they attended to the more youthful and rightful purveyors of the next generation. Finally, at 6 a.m. a nurse deigned to attend to her.

'My baby's arrived,' Mum said.

'Don't be ridiculous, mother,' the nurse said and walked away.

Mother screamed, the nurse acquiesced and pulled back the covers, to reveal me lying whimpering in the bed.

She was tough my mum; so must have been I, as I wasn't suffocated by the bedding. Premature by a month and just over 5lbs, I was installed in a cot next to her bed with two post office directories beneath the legs to increase the circulation to my head; the 1950s' East End version of paediatric care for the premature.

Visiting hours were defined and immutable but she knew that my grandmother Isabella was in the hospital long before she appeared. 'I heard her metal-tipped walking stick hitting the floor in the corridor, you could always tell when she was coming.'

In unison the two ward doors had flown open, and making the grandest of theatrical entrances in she strode.

Seventy-two years of age and eighteen stone in weight, dressed in a brightly coloured floral dress overlaid by a black woollen overcoat with fox fur collar, in a stentorian voice she demanded to see her daughter.

The ward sister bore down upon her like a tank; it was NOT visiting time. Nan apparently swatted her aside, having spotted Mum at the far end of the ward. I had been placed with her by the open window, in order that I could enjoy the fumes from the main road. I was small, ginger haired and very wrinkled.

Nan stripped back the blanket to observe her new grandchild. 'Is that all there is, Bella? Blimey, was it worth it?'

* * *

So little furniture do I have in my new home that the sun is still shining when I come to unpack my books and come across the medical dictionary, which was Mother's bible. It is dated 1946 and she used it whenever an illness or a diagnosis seemed to her unusual or worthy of note. It was second hand when she acquired it, having the name Hilda Johnson written in red on the inside cover; books, like many things, were a luxury Mum could ill afford. She got this when she worked at the children's hospital on Hackney Road, where she made the uniforms for the staff and briefly had a sideline in making shirts for the male doctors.

It's been a long day and I sit thankfully and skim through the adverts for Do-Do tablets for asthma and 'Roboleine – the food that builds the body'. I am especially taken by the section on 'Gas Warfare Precautions', something nursing staff surely have little need of today, in the 1980s. The thick squat pages bear the stains of god only knows what upon them. I come to a section I recall only too well. Under ear, it simply says 'the organ of hearing'.

* * *

At the age of four, I am blissfully unaware that both my mother and her mother, my nan, have a firm belief in home treatment for almost all ailments. That is, after all, all they had known until the establishment of the NHS a short four years before my birth. All that I know is that I am lying on a pillow on an armchair in the kitchen with a hazy awareness that Mum is flipping through the dictionary.

She looks at me once more. 'Only one ear hurts?' I point to the affected organ. 'All right then.'

Dad is seated opposite reading his newspaper as she bustles past and out into the scullery. I hear the sound of glass chinking on glass as she searches for whatever treatment she has decided upon. I would love to sleep, but the throbbing ear precludes that. That day I was lucky, there was no 30 per cent peroxide left, one of her standard treatments for everything. Her diagnosis for ears was almost always that wax was the culprit, but today, thwarted by the lack of serious chemicals, she bathes my inner ear in warm olive oil and gently massages behind it.

'Better?'

'No.'

As I lay there, my great-aunt Clara knocks on the kitchen door. She and my paternal grandmother, Alice, occupy three rooms upstairs and have done so since both they and my family had been bombed out of their homes during the war. Clara has a good heart and she has bought me a doll to replace Peggy, my favourite, who has suffered many assaults. Peggy's skull is held together with Sellotape and she has a black hole in the big toe of her right foot courtesy of an early experiment in smoking by my brother, Tony. All in all, she is a sorry sight.

The new doll on the other hand is exquisitely ugly. A kind of giant 1950s' Barbie, brash with bright-red lipstick and with a terrifying cry. One reason I love Peggy so much is that she is mute. Her soundbox, like much else about her, has ceased to work.

By now my ear is even more painful and I begin to cry. Clara is crestfallen, she thinks I hate the doll, which I do, but at that moment I just wanted the pain to go away.

It does go away, but only after a hefty dose of antibiotics. Mother finally acquiesces and rushes me to the evening session at the surgery, where the softly spoken Dr Marks declares that it is a bacterial infection. I don't know if Mum admits her attempts at home therapy to him, but I suspect he knows only too well that the locals practise it widely. Nan would have resorted to do-it-yourself surgery had she been able. Old habits die hard, but some ailments were beyond the realm of folk-medicine even for her.

The consulting room in which we sit has a surprising set of French windows which open onto a garden. You can hardly believe that you are on Hackney Road such elegance do they imply. Today, as it is winter, they are closed, but in summer the gossamer-thin white curtains which shield the room billow inwards, bringing with them the smell of roses which bloom outside in profusion. A gas heater in the corner warms the room as the doctor's black scribble makes its way across the page. He has a blotter on a handle which fascinates me. I long to ask him how many prescriptions he has to write before the paper is spent and needs replacing. He catches my eye and smiles. He is of Indian extraction and his tanned skin and pencil-straight moustache are a direct opposite to the colleague with whom he shares the surgery. Dr Rockveldt is from South Africa. He is large, white, bald and lugubrious, full of bonhomie and very popular with the older ladies.

Dr Marks blots his pad. 'I saw your mother today, Bella,' he said handing the script to Mum.

'Her heart?'

'Yes. I gave her some new pills. Keep an eye on her. She may dehydrate.'

'Is she worse?'

'Hard to say. She's no moaner.'

Mum nods and we venture out through a waiting room packed to standing, up a short flight of stairs onto the street and turn right.

The chemist shop we use is, like everything else around me, old. The wooden step you climb to enter is worn in the middle by a hundred years and more of the tread of customers. It sits on the corner of Hackney Road and Goldsmiths Row, which once boasted the eponymous alms houses but now has a run of tiny shops which you have to step down into to enter and in which the smell of damp is overwhelming. They house tailors and bootmakers and a pet shop dealing in cat meat.

Inside the pharmacy three bentwood chairs are lined up for people to sit upon while the medicines are made. There are no boxes or bottles of pills except aspirin and the most common medicaments. Shelves are lined with powdered chemicals which the pharmacist mixes and then pounds into tablets using metal pill-frames and what look like wide pestles. The smells in the shop are so complex that they send my head reeling.

I sit on Mum's lap as we wait our turn. In spite of the throbbing in my ear I am fascinated by the large glass bottles shaped like pears, known as show globes, that sit in the window. They are the only bit of colour on Hackney Road.

My medicine comes pre-made in liquid form in the usual brown bottle. Mum looks at it. 'It won't cause her trouble?'

This is a weighted question as my brother had had some of the earliest penicillin available as an injection, to which he had been wildly allergic.

'No, Mrs Wilkinson, that's been sorted out.'

She is placated and takes the brown paper bag in which Mr Davis has wrapped the bottle and puts it into her shopping bag.

He leans over the counter towards me. 'Linda, you must take the medicine, all of it. Promise me?'

I nod and he gives me a small piece of rock twisted inside cellophane. My ear hurts so much I cannot even think of sucking it. I am grateful for it later, though, as an antidote to the foul-tasting liquid that I have to swallow to get rid of the infection.

As soon as I feel a little better I remember the conversation Mum had with the doctor.

'What's dehydrate?'

She tells me and sighs, waiting for me to ask for more information.

'So why will Nan dry out?'

'Well, she's bloated, her heart isn't working well. Less fluid will be good for her.'

'Why?'

And so it goes on.

Mother hopes that she has discovered an antidote to my continually asking questions. Every weekday afternoon, she stops machining for an hour. She is a piece worker; paid by the number of garments she produces. At the moment it is men's waistcoats. I have learned to turn the small straps that she makes the right way out. Using a knitting needle I sit working on the floor by her feet as she machines at break-neck speed. We have some lunch and turn on the radio for 'Listen with Mother'. I sit at the kitchen table and relish the words that flow from the brown Bakelite box on the wall.

I hadn't spoken until late. Most of the family had thought that I was simple, but I am a watcher; something of a curse sometimes. I recall sitting staring at people and twisting one of the curls on my forehead around and around. Language that began in my head as a noise like bees in a hive had slowly organised itself into meaning and I began to speak.

Mother wasn't surprised, she always said that my actions weren't those of a simpleton.

The programme finishes and she gets out some sheets of paper. They are from the factory that supplies her with work and are sturdy and brown and used to make clothing patterns. On them the alphabet is written. From somewhere she has obtained a large tin of shells of all shapes and sizes which carry the smell of the sea. Some still have a patina of salt on their surface, others are smooth, but whatever their texture I use them to outline the letters Mum has written. I have moved beyond mere copying to making the sound of the letter as I go along. It is a system of her own devising and for me it works. She hopes that I will migrate from this on to simple books and then others that may contain the answers to the questions that I constantly ask of her.

'She was born asking why,' she tells Raphael Landau, the albino owner of the clothing factory for whom she works, as he drops off a pile of waistcoats to be made. He has the heavy features of the Middle European Jews, but his hair is white and his eyes so pale as to be transparent. He wants her to run his factory; she is not so sure that she wants to leave me to be looked after by Alice, Dad's mother.

'You'll earn a lot more,' he tells her, as I fiddle with the bundle of garments at his feet.

'Why?' I ask.

'See I told you, Rafe.'

'Because, girlie, your mum has the gift for making clothes and I need her.'

He turns to her. 'There's more work about, Bella, a lot more. Fashions are changing.'

I sense Mum is not impressed by his plea. 'Maybe in the future.'

He shrugs and drives off.

Mum looks after him anxiously. Rafe is completely colour blind, including to traffic signals.

We return to our weekday routines. Life is not driven by them, but guided in a seamless fashion by mother. We may not have a fridge or anything other than a cold water tap and an outside toilet, but in one respect we exhibit one of the highest achievements of civilisation, cleanliness. In order to avoid the nits, bugs, scabies and other afflictions that poverty brings with it, our ablutions are monitored by Mum with an almost clinical precision, and our laundry treated with a reverence some reserve only for god.

On a daily basis, coloured washing is done by hand and hung outside to dry, but there is one routine during the week which is sacrosanct, the day we visit the laundry at York Hall. With shopping trolleys bulging with anything that could be boiled, Mum, Nan and I walked the half-mile or so up Hackney Road then along Cambridge Heath Road to enter a haven of female fortitude.

The first thing that met your eyes was the colour white; sheets that were white. Heavy, strong cotton, capable of withstanding the pummel and grind of the wash. Able to hold and caress the bleach and steam, the mangle and the iron. You could smell the laughter and the pain of the women who turned the paddles and dropped the 'bluing' into the huge, bubbling cauldrons of water. Almost invisible in the mist, the women were mere ghosts to their echoing laughter. Heavy and huge the wheels of the mangles groaned and turned. Hot arms, aching backs and the drizzle of water onto the floor and all the time the conversation flowed: tales of love, lust and illness; tales of hopes, mostly dashed; tales. I would sit on one of the benches which lined the walls and listen, absorbing the emotions that flew around me. It was here that I first realised that I could feel through my skin. Not the pain of a cut or a bruise, but another kind of pain, that of other people's loss, or yearning for something which would never be. My forearms would tingle and I would know.

'Good riddance to bad rubbish,' someone would say on hearing a woman had been deserted by her husband. The woman would laugh in comradely agreement, coping as they all had to. My skin would scream in agony when she passed by or sat next to me, exhausted by the heat and life.

'Look at your nan,' they would often say, pointing.

And I would, her top peeled down, her naked bosoms hanging on her stomach as dripping in sweat she worked the mangle.

'They don't make them like that anymore.'

They were words of sheer admiration for someone who had survived.

The product of this labour of love takes centre stage on Sundays when those sheets in their recently reaffirmed virgin purity are laid anew onto the beds. Crisp and almost hard to the touch, they still smell of the laundry from whence they came. I am too small to help Mum, but I try as best I am able. Smooth, tuck and turn.

A single blanket and a candlewick cover; it is summer. 'That's better,' Mum says, observing what to her is a work of art.

Sunday has its own rhythm and rites. After the changing of the beds Mum will check that the roast is ready for the oven that the vegetables are prepared and she will, for the first time that week, sit and read a newspaper. If the weather is fine in mid-morning Nan will visit for a cup of tea, but irrespective at noon Dad will go to the pub and come home for his meal and an afternoon sleep.

Over and above all of this, the Sunday flower market takes place as it has done since the 1860s. I adore the fact that I can perch on the doorstep and watch the ebb and flow of people. Women wear the ubiquitous turbans over their hair as they purchase flowers, or bulbs. Not many men are out apart from the market traders who flirt mercilessly with the clientele, who give as good back. The hue and cry of the costers in the market is the same as many another. 'So many for two and six,' the numbers a moveable feast according to the season. 'The best bargain you'll ever have.' Goods are sold from the pavement, having come on handcarts or in small vans. It feels warm and safe and happy, and I hug my knees and relish the entertainment.

My grandmother is upon me before I realise it. Wearing her best dress she prods me with her walking stick. Her soft white hair is piled ornately under a pearl-encrusted hairnet and outrageous earrings dance and dangle with her every movement. She is in her late seventies and she scares most people. 'Get up dreamer, let me by.' She pats me none too softly on the head and wanders down the passageway.

In the kitchen, I occupy my favourite spot on the floor where I can appreciate the enormity of both Nan and her personality. I love these visits.

I see her on Saturdays when we go to her flat near the Broadway Market to do her shopping, but having her here in my home feels special. I watch as she pours tea into her saucer, dunks toast into the cup and then sucks it. She has teeth, false teeth, but they sit in a handkerchief in her coat pocket. The slurping sound as she sucks the tea from the saucer is unrestrained.

'Mum!'

'I can't wear the teeth all the time Bella, they rub.'

Dad, who is ever present at these visits, rattles his newspaper but remains invisible behind it.

'Get some new ones.'

Nan seems fond of her black rubber dentures, but perhaps it's just that she hasn't got the hang of a new pair being free on the State.

'Lin's going to nursery soon,' Mum informs her.

'She'll have to speak then.'

'I can speak.'

'Can you now?'

'And she can read.'

'Don't be daft, she's only a child.'

'Mum taught me.'

She is unimpressed until Mother snatches the newspaper from Dad and I stutter through a few sentences.

'She's a strange one, all that staring at you in silence, now this.'

'She's just a bit different.'

They drift on to conversations not connected with me and I slip back into watching them. Tony, my brother, comes in; he and Nan have a great affection for one other. He is full of the bustle of a teenager on his way to manhood and I have to sit on a chair to avoid his stomping feet. Even Dad lowers his paper and joins in until twelve o'clock chimes. Nan leaves, Dad changes to go to the pub and Mum returns to the kitchen.

Later, once Dad has returned and eaten his roast, he falls asleep on the smooth white territory of the bed where I join him. Mother sits and snoozes in the kitchen, legs propped on another chair, but Dad and I lie down. He has a smell on these afternoons, a smell that I can never forget. In contrast to the sheets it is a feast of the earth. Sweat, beer and tobacco. In his armpits the black mat of hairs curl, unlike the dark straightness on his head. There is no grey there, well, perhaps a hint. Sunlight is deflected by the window of the house next door. It bounces weakly into the bedroom. The walnut veneer of the bedhead is warmed to a deep glow. I trace the black lines with a small finger. Soon he will have to wake. Soon the beer will clear from his head. It will be six o'clock and we will eat winkles, shrimps and white buttered bread. Later he will stand in the street, this summer street, and smoke in the darkness. I will sit on the window ledge next to him and listen to the soft banter that the neighbours exchange. There is no traffic and the other children race up and down. He knows that I prefer to sit close to him; there are never any admonishments to go and play.

I kneel on the bed and look down at him. The vest and pants he wears are thick. Like the sheets they have survived the passage through the inferno of cleaning. Above the bed, behind the walnut, is a mantelpiece. On this stands a glass of water. I hear sounds of stirring and a kettle being filled. Gently I dip a comb into the glass. The drips fall like small crystals as I drag the teeth slowly through his hair. His eyes like mine are brown. Smiling, he stays my hand.

'All right, kid?' I nod, and he envelopes me in a glorious hug of love and understanding.

Chapter 2

Great-Aunt Clara

I slowly become aware Carol is standing next to me sorting through some of her books.

'What's that?' she asks, pointing at the medical dictionary.

I toss it to her; she catches it and flicks through the pages. 'It was Mum's.'

'You were miles away.'

'I'm tired.'

We are both tired; we need a meal and a sleep. We only have a single bed, which at the moment sits in the lounge doubling up as a sofa. Sleeping will not be comfortable.

'Food?'

She nods.

The evening continues to be glorious as I walk her the back way to Bethnal Green Road to the Venus Kebab House, home to the East End Mafia if you are able to visit at 2 a.m.

It is a large and dark establishment, taking up two former shops; a classic cliché-ridden Greek restaurant full of tacky memorabilia and posters.

The food, though, is as good as I recall it being when my parents and I had gone there. The wine is an excellent but surprisingly inexpensive St Emilion, which merits a second bottle.

It is a soft night and as we navigate the path home the air is suddenly heavy with the scent of a jasmine bush in full bloom, whose flowers have cascaded over a garden wall and onto the street. As we enter the small estate of cottages on which we now live, she squeezes my arm.

'It's not beautiful?' I say pre-empting her.

'No, but here we are.'

'Make the best of it?'

'How long?'

'. . . will we be living here?'

'No. Before you tell me why we are here at all?'

'It makes sense, you agreed that much.'

She cuddles into me. 'It does, but give me credit for knowing you.'

'The call of the familiar,' I say.

'What's that?' she asks pointing upwards.

The outlet from the factory on Wimbolt Street sits proudly and functionally above us.

'Wood dust,' I say.

She ignores me, too much wine and emotion have won the day, and we walk home in a companionable silence not matched by the scenes that are playing in my mind.

* * *

'Wood dust.'

The dray horses and the cart which they pull have just gone, leaving steamy stools on the road outside of The Royal Oak pub, two doors down from where I live. The athletic throw, thump and roll of the beer barrels has entertained

me, particularly the precision with which they hit the thick
hessian rug which halts their trajectory before they are
rolled into the basement. To my child's eye the dung the
horses have left behind have elements of hessian in them,
shards of hay and hessian look very similar after all. I don't
prod, just stare at their strange roundness.

Columbia Road is alive with sounds and smells, some
from near, some afar. Most mornings, whatever the direction the wind, the odour of brewing hops from Truman's
brewery on Brick Lane coats us in a heady fug. The boot
menders, Daltrey's, at number 148, has a small burner,
over which hangs a pot of glue whose smell in summer
wafts onto the street and in winter, when the door is closed,
almost asphyxiates you on entry. Above all is the constant
thrum of the sawmills as wood is cut, turned, and then
fashioned into furniture in the factories that pepper the
area. French polishing adds another olfactory assault to the
neighbourhood, but I am so used to it to be almost oblivious. Nobody is oblivious to the wood dust, which coats
everything. Filters are unheard of, apart from tying a sack
over the outlet chimney on the roof from time to time. At
busy periods the dust drifts in the street creating a kind of
East End desert.

On one such a day I look up from the sawdust dune that
I have assembled in the gutter and, through the haze of
particles dancing in the sunlight, I see three silhouetted
forms coming towards me. They appear to be performing
a macabre dance. At the speed of a pavane my great-
aunt Clara, supported by two female neighbours, lurches

towards the front door of our house, number 77. The door is open and somehow the women bundle her inside, down the passageway and up the stairs.

It transpired that Clara had a secret; for all I know she had many, but one in particular had brought her to have the stroke which destroyed her on that sunny late summer's day. She had lost her job filling bags of sugar at the factory at Canning Town. The job had been lost many weeks before her illness, but, being the sole bread-winner of the unit that was she and Alice, she was riven with shame. Each day she had gone out as if going to work. She had trudged the streets, had cups of tea and sat on park benches, the like of which she was found on in Ion Square weeping and caterwauling. She had gone through what little savings she had and was terrified of telling Alice, with whom she had a love–hate relationship of dependency.

Having been born in 1903 Clara was one of the genera-tion for whom marriage was an unobtainable dream. While the paucity of men post First World War was one factor, the other was that she was sadly not attractive. She'd had a beau at one time, a man by whom she was 'courted', but that came to nothing. She was essentially alone and very lonely. When I was born she had lavished presents upon me and spent hours and hours cuddling me. In the end, Dad had asked her to just '*pop*' in after work for a quick cup of tea, to give the family some space. Getting Dad to do anything was an accomplishment on Mother's part, but as Clara was his aunt she was his responsibility. The rift had hurt Clara, as I was the only point of physical contact she had.

The distance which existed between her and my family was something that I divined through my skin. Unspoken but ever present, it literally made my arms tingle. I didn't know what had caused it until later, but because of the effect the situation had on me she was someone I had learned to be cautious of.

The upstairs window of the bedroom that Alice, my grandmother, and Clara shared was open, and screaming began to emanate from it. Panic-stricken, the helpful neighbours fled down the stairs and out of the house. They stood at the corner of the street where an inquisitive huddle of passers-by soon formed. I crept up the stairs to see Alice smashing Clara about the head with a shoe. Almost synchronously my mother appeared and together we pulled Alice off the stricken woman who lay prostrate on the bed.

'Lazy, lazy cow,' Alice shouted. 'Why weren't you at work?'

Mother was looking at Clara. 'Shut up Al, for goodness' sake look at her.'

I'd sidled around to my great-aunt and taken her hand. Her face looked as if a landslide had occurred. One single huge tear was making its way down her face. I should have been at school that day, but Mother liked to have me at home with her on the Jewish holidays when Rafe's factory, in which she now worked, closed.

Soon after an ambulance came to take Clara away. It was a difficult prospect as she was now immobile and distraught. The two ambulance men strapped her into a carry chair and bumped her slowly down the narrow stairs. She was crying profusely.

Those few weeks she was away were peaceful. I suppose that was because Alice more or less lived with my aunt Lillie. I also realised that our home was ours for the first time. There was a sense of calm about the house that I had never known before. There was even talk that, if things went 'well', I might have my own bedroom and not sleep in with my parents.

Things went 'well' for nobody, sadly. When Clara returned from her sojourn in hospital she could not speak and walking was a major exercise. As we had only a downstairs toilet out in the yard, life became difficult for her. I have often wondered why we didn't reverse the living arrangements, but I suspect the levels of resentment rendered that impossible.

Alice had lost her husband in the first war and had survived by taking in washing, so her life had been far from easy. Her one delight was a visit to the pub next door but one, The Royal Oak, where she and a bunch of local ladies would imbibe Guinness in some volume. She was therefore a regular of the Mildmay Mission Hospital's accident department, as the five yards home were often far more than she could manage. I recall one night finding her lying in the gutter outside home, her lip split from an encounter with the kerb. Another time she actually made it into the house, to collapse on the stairs, where she gave my brother the contents of her purse as he was, 'Such a good boy.' Sometimes when waking up in the hospital to see the nursing sisters with their starched white headgear, she would flee the hundred yards home barefoot, convinced she was dead and awaiting judgment.

Mum and Dad both worked so I was left in Alice's care and she would, from time to time, walk me to and from school to ensure that I was safe. *I* was safe, from physical harm, perhaps.

Sometimes when I dream I still see the hand rising in slow motion. It was neither a dull day, nor sunny; neither winter nor summer, but that in-between time of year, when it began. Clara was sitting in her armchair by the bedroom window. I saw her follow the trajectory of the hand with her eyes. All that escaped her lips was a gasp as the full open-handed slap reverberated through her head. Alice, who was unconscious of anything except her own anger, turned on her heel and stormed out, leaving Clara a quivering wreck. Hardly a glance was spent on me who, freshly home from school, stood in the doorway. Clara's hand was cold and clammy when I took it. She was struggling to speak and spittle glimmered on her hirsute chin as she fought to find the word. In a howl a sound which may have been 'sorry' erupted into the air.

I sat on a footstool and tried to comfort her tears. All thought of any distance between us evaporated as I watched her try to control her fear. Was it the first time she had been assaulted? I doubt it.

In the kitchen, Alice was boiling a kettle on her stove as if nothing had happened, a glass of milk stood waiting for me on the table next to a couple of biscuits. I climbed up onto a chair and ate and drank in silence. I'd like to say that she said something, that she was contrite, but she didn't and wasn't.

Sometimes it felt as if a lifetime's rage against the world and the circumstances of her own life were focused on the bedraggled immobile form of Clara, who would huddle down to avoid the blows that would increasingly rain down upon her.

At first I would try to hide downstairs, waiting for Mum to come home from work. Then one day I saw Alice throw a milk bottle at Clara; it caught her on the forehead with a thump.

'Stupid bitch. Useless, useless!' Alice was shouting.

'Stop it, leave her alone!'

Blood was trickling from Clara's wound. Alice turned to me, a flicker of something passed behind her eyes. 'She tripped over.'

I shook my head, and time elongated as we stared at one another. An eight-year-old child and a seventy-eight-year-old, arthritic woman, related by blood but seemingly nothing more.

I could hear Clara whimpering, by now the blood had reached her mouth and she licked at it. She was confused and afraid. Alice looked at her and bustled away, returning with a rag and a bottle of iodine. At Alice's approach Clara tried to disappear into the wall behind her, but almost gently Alice bathed the wound, cooing as she might with a child.

I sensed that the attacks would continue, I also sensed that she would lie her way out of them if I told on her. I had but one option it seemed, to protect Clara myself. I have wondered many a time from where this attitude came, the belief that I could change the situation, alter the course of a life. I had no idea then, and I am not any nearer to understanding it now.

I approached Clara's well-being like a military campaign. I had to make her well and happy and that meant sorting out some practicalities.

My logic was that if I were with her as much as possible that would keep Alice at bay. She never to my knowledge hit Clara when my parents or Tony were in the house. I couldn't do anything about my school time but whenever I could I would play in the bedroom which they shared. My cousin David had a large set of lead army figurines and we would devise complex battles with these all over the room. Clara would feast her eyes on the colours and chuckle at our lengthy discussions and arguments about the pros and cons of various positions.

One day, when I sat reading a schoolbook, she pointed and I passed it to her.

A string of distorted sounds came from her lips. She smiled at me, she could read! I gave her a newspaper, she shook her head, the type was too small.

I began my campaign to get Clara glasses by telling Mum that she could read. I hoped that she would be the weak link in the antipathy that the family seemed to have towards their stroke-ridden relative. Mum told Aunt Lillie of my discovery, and she came over to watch Clara's attempts at reading. Between them they decided that it would be good if she were tested. It might stop her sitting crying out for most of the day, they concluded.

The optician was a lovely man who translated Clara's grunts almost as well as I had come to, and somehow managed to get her prescription, if not perfect, then adequate enough.

Alice had stayed out of all of this, she was sure that nothing was worth the effort where Clara was concerned. She and I had developed an uneasy truce. She knew full well why I was so present in their lives. If anybody noticed the froideur between us they never said, and after all everyone knew that I was an odd child, something which in this situation played in my favour.

Clara now sat happily reading. For the first time since her stroke she was a person again, although her small round glasses, gratis from the NHS, did little to improve her looks. Never a beauty, she was a lumpen mass of fat, encased in dresses made by my aunts, her nieces. Her hair was lank, thin, grey and greasy, and her dental hygiene non-existent. I tackled this full-on with Alice. I had saved up and got Clara a toothbrush, but she couldn't manage the motion to clean her teeth, it was a two-person job. I know that she didn't think it worth the effort, but by this point she would do anything to please me, to keep me in her life.

I distinctly recall standing in Alice's kitchen and shouting for her help. For a brief moment I thought she was going to use the knife with which she was peeling potatoes on me. She had small dark eyes and they glinted with both confusion and anger.

'Leave it, can't you?'

I shook my head and pointed to the toothbrush. She held a terrified Clara's mouth open while I stood on a stool and tried as best I could to clean her rotting teeth. It was to be a losing battle.

Once Clara had knitted for the whole family and I wondered if she could still wield needles. She could, but reading patterns was beyond her. No matter, she would knit endless scarves with holes in them which gave her great joy. They became the staple of my Christmas presents to the family.

During this whole period nobody from the health professions came to see her. There was no follow-up home care, or if there was nobody had suggested it, so despite my attempts to help, her slow and inevitable decline went unnoticed by the authorities.

My parents became aware of my obsession, and by now a vocal nine-year-old, the rows that I had with Alice about Clara were an unwelcome feature of our lives. They decided that Aunt Lillie would look after me during term time and that I would spend my school holidays with Nan, my other grandmother.

Chapter 3

Nan

Until then, apart from her Sunday visits, my interactions with Nan had been clothed in the unspoken animosity that lay between her and my mother, something I hadn't had to pick up via my skin, it was so obvious when it was just the three of us together. On Saturdays, for as long as she was able, Nan came with us to do her shopping in the Broadway Market. Here she was treated like royalty. She'd lived there for years before moving to her flat on the Dinmont Estate, just off Hackney Road.

Old neighbours and all of the stallholders knew her. She never bought fruit without savouring it first; nobody minded but my mother. Nan would stand and chat while eating a grape or a cherry. She loved stone fruit; damson plums were her favourite. I emulated her once or twice to have Mum slap my hand and take the fruit away.

'Mum!'

'They're not yours until you've paid for them,' she'd say.

Nan would stoically ignore her remark and continue plucking fruit from the stalls.

'Sets her a bad example,' she'd opine later.

'Tosh,' Nan would say.

*

Nan never told me why she so freely regaled herself of produce, but one of the costers told me after she had died. During the late 1920s there had been a TB outbreak on Ada Street where Nan and her family had lived. Nan, and the grandfather I never knew, had taken in the orphans of parents who had died from it on the street and fed and cared for them. Two, Rosie and Artie, had even been unofficially adopted by the family. It was an act of selflessness which ended in my grandfather dying of TB himself in 1932, although it was so prevalent that he may well have suffered from it anyway. People have long memories for deeds of that nature, selflessly performed. Mum must have known about it, but never discussed it.

We'd finish our visit to the market with a plate of eels and mash in Cooke's Pie and Eel Shop with its marble tables, bent cutlery and sawdust strewn floor. Outside of the shop was the eel stall where the squirming fish sat in trays, defined by their size in circumference. Served by the pound, their heads were unceremoniously chopped off on a wooden board to fall onto the street below, where a tribe of happy cats gorged themselves stupid. When I was very young, Nan would pop into the Sir Walter Scott pub by the Regent's Canal for a pint of Guinness before she went home, something else which embarrassed Mum, who would never join her.

We'd drop Nan's shopping trolley off in her flat so that, no matter how many pints she'd consumed, she'd arrive home to find her purchases already safely stowed away.

Mum would often pause and look at the photographs so lovingly displayed on every surface of the front room by this mother she seemed not to like very much. There was only one shot of my grandfather. A black-haired Welshman who'd sported a moustache to cover his harelip. The photograph was posed and had been taken in a studio. He sat in profile, sporting a flat cap, so that any expression was unreadable. I knew that he had been short, played the penny whistle and the Jew's harp, and danced the jig. He had marched his children up and down the yard in formation, trying to drill a discipline into them that he never exhibited himself.

Mum had never lived in the flat that Nan now occupied. Having married my father in 1939 she'd gone from Ada Street to Baxendale Street, just around the corner from Columbia Road. Soon afterwards Ada Street had been cleared of houses and along with them went the rats which had terrorised Mum's childhood. Her back was riven with scars where one had leapt onto her while she was having a strip wash in the kitchen. Using her skin as an anchor it had slid down in order to reach the floor and escape.

It was the summer holidays and I'd been with Nan for almost a fortnight, during which neither of us seemed to have put a foot wrong with Mother. I was dropped off when Mum went to work and picked up on the way home. For the first few days Mum had come over at lunchtime to eat with us, but Nan had told her that it wasn't necessary, I was a model child. I sensed though that it had never been me that Mum was concerned about.

At Nan's, I never played with other children. There were plenty running around outside and screaming up and down the corridors, but Nan never suggested I go and play with them and I never asked. She would stand me on a beer crate and get me to butter bread, or instruct me on the right way to souse a herring or cook a kipper. Hot buttery kippers and bread to mop up the juice were a great favourite. We'd sit and suck and chew, happily washing them down with milk for me, beer for her.

One day at noon she put on her outdoor clothes and took me on an 'outing' to a nearby pub.

'Our copy-book is clean my girl; let's make the most of it,' she said, adjusting her hairnet in the mirror.

It was the first of many such visits to that bar where the cigarette smoke was so thick that you could have cut it with a blunt knife leaving a slash that lasted minutes. I would watch in fascination as the smoke wafted upwards white and grey, like a tired hurricane, circling slowly to end as a yellow plume resting edgily under the glow of a spotlight.

There was a stage at one end of the pub which, like the floor, was covered with linoleum. At some time it had worn a pattern in shades of green, but now its edges were eroded and its surface pockmarked by cigarette burns and the scuff of heels. Nan held my hand fast as we crossed the threshold, children were not allowed in pubs, but I was hers. A murmur went up and a clutch of greetings were uttered. Nothing was said of my presence and soon a pattern to these afternoons was established. Someone would reach down, pick me up and seat me on the bar.

The out of tune piano would play for some time and then Nan would rise. She was through the smoke an unexpected dash of colour and movement, gliding towards the stage with a grace which belied her size. In a single movement, she removed her beloved false teeth, burying them deep into the pockets of her pinafore, and nodded to the pianist. I suppose that she must have been eighty at the time. Her age, like much about her, was wedged in the folklore of the area. Even to me she looked faintly ridiculous, a worn old woman; until she sang. Her voice, a shadow of a once powerful instrument, caressed softly the notes of a blues number. With her eyes closed she transported herself back to the time when she had truly earned her beer with her voice. Yet even now cigarettes came to rest like an array of twinkling stage lights as the customers listened. They weren't an audience from whom you would expect such attention, workers at lunchtime, men over their hard-earned pint.

When she had finished, had responded to the cries of, 'Come on Bella, give us another,' for as long as she was able, we would go home.

Using me as a walking stick, our uneven procession ended at the bottom of a mountain. Two flights of urine-sodden concrete steps which always smelt of yesterday's overcooked cabbage. 'Go up,' she would say, breathlessly handing me the key to her flat. 'Put the kettle on, there's a love.'

Finally, when the steam had been gushing for many minutes, Nan shuffled in, wheezing and gasping to settle down for her cup of tea and her snooze. Our lunchtime adventures in the Sebright Arms were our secret. Mother already had enough reservations about Nan caring for me without finding out that I spent my school holidays polishing glasses and emptying ashtrays in a pub.

Once Nan had settled into her armchair and the snoring had begun I was free to roam. The flat had two bedrooms, one where my uncle Ted slept, the other hers. It was to this perfumed boudoir that I retired until time was ripe to waken her. The baubles and bangles attested to her flamboyance, and the faded old photos from the turn of the century to her time on the music hall boards. Smiling, huge in girth and dressed to the nines, she and her sister, Charlotte, looked down on the room. They had worked the boards, mostly at The Empire in Shoreditch, until Charlotte's marriage. Nan told me little of those days. Born into the slums of London in 1880, or thereabouts, the grinding poverty in which she had lived can hardly have been a pleasant memory.

One day I developed a toothache. Sitting at her old gate-leg table, my reading of the newspaper out loud was punctuated by a series of dribbles onto the typeface. I could sense Nan's frustration as my pronunciation degenerated into nonsense. She couldn't read and I was her lifeline to the world.

'What's up?' she asked, none too pleasantly.

'It's me tooth, Nan, it's all swollen.'

'Show me.' Bending over she yanked my head, with attached neck, nearer her eyes.

'Open your mouth,' she said, peering and poking in unison at the afflicted tooth which throbbed beneath her finger. 'Soon fix that.'

Muttering, she opened the wooden, panelled cupboard which housed just about everything from Alka-Seltzer to a shoe horn, and, with reverence, extracted an old bottle. It was one of a type I had seen on display at the local chemist as a container from a bygone age; small, squat and brown, with a plug-in glass stopper. The label, presumably once white, was aged to an amber colour, enhanced by runnels of past pourings over its surface. It seemed empty; Nan was annoyed. The dull sucking sound of her tongue against the roof of her toothless mouth indicated deep thought. Eventually, a wide grin erupted and she winked down at me. 'Don't worry. Soon pep it up.'

'Pepping it up' involved mixing a small amount of gin with the solidified goo at the bottom of the vial. I stood in the kitchen on the beer crate which doubled as my stool as she repeatedly immersed the bottle into hot water, working at the mixture with a thin-handled spoon, her fat arms flapping like bellows with the effort.

'That's it, good as new. Suck on this, push it over the tooth what hurts.' The sodden wad of cotton wool felt cold, then strangely warm, against my gum.

'Go in the front room and sit down, it'll soon be better.'

The warmth from the pad electrified my mouth, coasted down my arms, through my abdomen and into my legs. I sat on the floor, a molten mass of colours, and tried to focus on my jigsaw puzzle. The rain on the grimy window became a kaleidoscope of dancing rainbows, while a voice pierced the glow.

'Good stuff that, don't know why there was all that fuss about it; never did me no harm. How's the tooth?'

I looked up, she was drinking a cup of Guinness. I managed a nod before the world of light took me away. I remember going into her bedroom while she slept, and playing with a string of pearls as I had a hundred times before. Only they weren't the same, each orb had both a huge halo around it, and a new clarity as if etched from ice. I held the strand up to the window where it became a waterfall which flowed through my fingers and down onto the bed, where I finally slept.

Next day I pulled a chair over to the cupboard and found the bottle. The letters were faded to a pale grey, 'Tincture of laudanum'. It was much later when I read *The Picture of Dorian Gray* that I understood exactly what I had been given.

Summer was the best, we could get out of the flat. Rather than me for support she would use an old pushchair; my shoulders could only carry her so far. When it was warm we would make it to the first bench in London Fields and sit. There was a children's play area which I was never allowed near. The local dogs viewed the sandpit as their very own territory and the sand itself had long moved on from golden yellow to sludgy brown. I was never distressed at not flying through the air on a swing or pitching off the roundabout. The slats of the wooden seat irritated my bum, but I never moved. If I sat and waited I knew that, eventually, she would talk, not the ramblings of an old woman, but a kind of directed storytelling. She wanted to teach me, share with me her version of life.

In those days she was substantial. Sitting back and squinting at the trees, she resembled a floral East End Buddha. We would look up at the patterns of the clouds, sometimes in silence, sometimes commenting on their resemblance to people we knew, or those she had known.

It was here that I learned that her mother, my great-grandmother, had fallen asleep on Nan's first children, twins, in a drunken stupor and smothered them to death. The mark of the blade with which Nan had tried to cut her own throat in grief was still, even now, evident. Here that she told me of the death and destruction of two world wars, of the Blitz, of humour and of love.

'This bomb went off, and we was all in this Anderson shelter. It had brick either end and corrugated iron over it. Well we was trapped, the door blocked off by this pile of rubble. I heard old Bill Joyce outside ask if there's anyone alive. "'Course I bleedin' am, and the rest of us too."

'He was a bright one Bill, he picks a small hole in the brick and asks me to try and climb through. Head first I goes, the hole was just big enough for me arms and shoulders, 'course being big I got stuck, so three of them pulls me and all the rest of the bricks out. I had them bruises for weeks.'

The veracity of her stories was always borne out by others, yet she lied. True they had pulled her thus through the brickwork, but at her suggestion, because a gas leak in the vicinity threatened to blow them all to kingdom come and there had been a baby in the shelter, and children to her were the source of light in the world.

More than relating her version of the past she tried to indoctrinate me with her version of life and how it should be lived. 'You mustn't be like your mum, afraid of your own shadow. Always trying to do the right thing. There's no such thing, you can't live by a set of rules, it just happens to you. Like the pub, what harm does it do? You earn a few bob, get all the crisps you want, but she wouldn't see it like that.'

'But she loves you, Nan.'

'I know, but she don't understand. How could she, she hasn't lived my life. You can't always be respectable, sometimes you have to fight, break the law even.'

She had been in jail twice, once in each of the world wars. Authority held little mystique for her; it was only in place, she knew, to protect the privileged from those such as herself. Had she not earned the nickname of 'Bella the basher', my mother could have forgiven her transgressions, after all she had been playing Robin Hood. When she told the tale her eyes would glaze over and she was once more that woman of thirty-seven with eight children, all of whom were cold.

'It was a bitter November that one of 1917. We'd burnt everything you could, some had even started on their furniture. I was coming down Brick Lane when I sees him, a young chap driving a coal cart all loaded up. He stops outside a pub and starts to unload. "It's all right for them as has," I thought. Then it came to me, I should nick the cart. He was a bit too quick, or me a bit too slow, 'cause he caught me untying the reins from the lamppost.

'"Listen," I says, "I don't want no trouble, but I'm taking it, there's them as needs it more."

'He didn't like that and tries to grab the reins, silly sod; so I lays him out flat, broke his nose. I'd never driven a horse and cart before, lucky he knew how to go in a straight line, 'cause I didn't.'

By the time the authorities had caught her, most of the coal had disappeared, and she had entered folk legend.

She insisted on keeping a pile of coal in her bath as what I assumed was a memento mori. As much as anything I assumed that she kept it to annoy my mother who, try as she might, could not persuade Nan on the possible joys of having a bath. After her death we found a neatly wrapped pile of gold sovereigns beneath the coal, her own personal bank ready for any emergency.

Our secret life together ended abruptly during the Easter break when I was nine. One of the men from the factory in which Mum worked sometimes came to the Sebright for lunch. She overheard him recounting the tale of an old woman who sang with a kid in tow.

I was happily kicking my heels against the bar to one of Nan's upbeat numbers when Mum arrived. Suddenly I was grabbed and whisked out into the alleyway. Her eyes, a hazel version of Nan's green, were manic as she shook me repeatedly. 'How long has this been going on, tell me? Tell me?'

Subconsciously I heard the singing stop way before Nan appeared. 'Leave her alone, she's only a child.'

They faced one another. 'If she's only a child what's she doing here, you stupid old woman?'

'Listen love, she's got to learn.'

'Learn what? About your bloody pride, an old wreck who still thinks she's something?'

I heard the groan of disapproval from the audience assembled inside the doorway.

'Christ, you give my arse a toothache. I may be an old wreck but at least I was something once. More than I can say for some,' Nan spat out with venom.

'Have it your way. But she's not ending up as a bar floozy or worse. Come on.'

I spent the rest of the afternoon filling in dockets at Mum's firm, hoping that the storm was over. It wasn't.

My mother's antipathy to pubs and alcohol I knew came from the fact that my grandfather, her father, had been an alcoholic. As a child I couldn't digest this as a problem as everyone around me drank. He, though, could not live without it. In the 1930s, when he was ill with TB and was sent to a sanatorium in Hastings to recuperate, he had climbed over the locked fence of the place in order to go to a pub. He had been found unconscious lying in the gutter and sent home post-haste. When Nan had tried to stop his intake of beer he had complied and stayed at home rather than visit a pub, but only because he had alcohol stashed all over the house, even up the chimney. When drunk he'd dive into the Regent's Canal from the Cat and Mutton Bridge, almost killing himself in the shallow waters. He worked the late shift as a printer on the *Morning Star* newspaper and would roll home inebriated at all hours, and so it went on.

Once he'd been introduced to a woman by one of his pals and had been seen 'canoodling' with her in the Walter Scott. Nan had stormed in, separated them and thrown the pal through the plate glass window onto the street. The fights and tears which Mum had experienced as home life between her parents were imprinted heavily on her mind. Little wonder she was sure that no child of hers was going to be exposed to that lifestyle. The upshot of this was that the next day I was back with Aunt Lillie, banned from spending too much time with Clara, and left to my own devices on the street.

Chapter 4

Diamond Lil

Of all the Lils who populated the East End, one in particular lives on in legend. As different from Ginger Lil, or my aunt Lillie in every way, Diamond Lil lit up many of the darker days of my childhood and I awaited her daily appearances with anticipation. If I sat on our doorstep and waited long enough she would appear. There was no regularity to Lil's morning procession down the street. It depended, I learned, on how late she had gone to bed the night before. Her blonde hair would be wrapped in an ornate turban, her slippers were always immaculately outrageous and, for a while, she had carried beneath her arm Fang, the miniature poodle who wore more faux jewellery than Lil did at that time of day.

I would run over and hover by the door as she entered the paper shop to collect her copy of the *Daily Mirror*. The owners had placed a stool near the counter upon which she would perch and regale them with tales of her nights singing in the pubs and clubs of the East End. Lil had a very long cigarette holder which she used as a baton to accompany her performance, the smoke from the cigarette tracing complex patterns in the air as she spoke. She was exciting, entrancing and wonderful. The world around us was pock-marked with bombsites, our homes blackened by a century of soot and smog, but amid this was Lil, the one piece of true glamour on the street.

One day I came home from school with a black eye. Mother treated it with witch hazel, goodness knows why. I suppose the pain was supposed to ensure that I didn't fight again, and indeed it was eye-wateringly awful.

'What happened?'

'Some boy at school said Lil was a bloke, so I bopped him one.'

'And he bopped you back?'

I nodded.

Mum sat me on a kitchen chair and sat opposite taking my hands in hers. Her look was concerned as she conjured her words with care. 'Lil is a man love.'

'No she's not.'

'She's really called Harry Young.'

I refused to believe her. How could that gilded creature be like my dad or brother? How could Lil have honed the sharp edges of manhood into the soft curves of womanhood?

'Ask your grandmother Isabella if you don't believe me,' Mum said kindly.

I knew that Nan sang with Lil in some of the pubs and I knew that she would tell me, but I wouldn't be seeing her until Saturday which was almost a week away. I stared at Mum, who by now understood that she would have to tell me otherwise I would pick at it like a sore.

Lil had always been there on the street; like Ginger Lil

her almost namesake, she was part of the architecture of life. I had sometimes noticed people snigger as she passed, but had assumed that it was jealousy at her startling looks and sashaying hips.

Mum had been told that until 1924 Lil had been plain old Harry, a fourteen-year-old teenage boy with scuffed knees and a snotty nose.

'Then, as the legend went, on the final day at school Harry came back after lunch dressed as a woman. He'd been secretly buying women's clothes for ages, and prancing about at home in high heels and dresses when everyone was out.'

Mum paused, unsure as to how to proceed. I give her credit for carrying on.

'See love, Lil likes men. There's people who are like that.'

I asked, 'Why?'

She shook her head. 'I don't know. I doubt if Lil does. Still there's no harm in her and she's a kindly soul.'

On this point I had to agree, but from then on I watched her more acutely and I noticed that her voice was that of a man's. It was the one thing she never disguised.

She lived in Guinness Buildings on Columbia Road with her partner Maisie, only of course nobody would have used that phrase back then. I suppose I should have realised that all was not as it seemed, that Lil was not our own local Lana Turner, by observing Maisie.

Chalk and cheese comes to mind. Whereas Lil was statuesque and beautiful, Maisie was anything but, and in drag she was a joke. Short, rotund and with an ability to put on lipstick reminiscent of a car crash, she would mince along the street. Rather than the elegant high heels that Lil wore, Maisie chose plimsolls that were held on with elastic bands. Many years later an aunt told me how she had once seen Maisie plying for trade at Liverpool Street Station, directly opposite Bishopsgate police station.

'Wasn't that dangerous?' I asked. 'Given that homosexuality was illegal.'

'Don't be daft,' she replied. 'Everyone knew Maisie would get no tricks. The police ignored her, would have been a waste of their time to bother.'

Maisie when he was George was a talented French polisher and must have passed as straight because he'd been in the services. Lil had tried to enlist during the war, but unable to eschew make-up, twinset and pearls had not gotten in. Lucky for the area she hadn't, because she kept morale up during the darkest hours. Many a serviceman from overseas who stumbled into London's East End for entertainment had a tale to tell, or a secret to keep, after meeting her. At the war's end, Lil had taken a beer crate around the streets upon which she would stand and sing her signature tune, 'I Want a Boy', to all and sundry for beer money.

* * *

I found this out some half a century later when researching a book about the area. One of my interviewees, who was eleven years old at war's end, had witnessed this scene. She sang a few phrases from the song to me but had no idea from whence it came.

Later, I wrote a musical about Lil and wondered if I would be able to track down the song. I held out little hope as I emailed the music section of the British Library. I had only the word of an old lady of something she'd heard a lifetime ago, and she may have confused it with one of a myriad of other memories that she had gathered throughout her life. But almost by return of mail a researcher at the library said he'd located it. The next day a copy of the song arrived through my letterbox. It was from 1920 and is as outrageous as Lil was. The opening lines were, 'I want a boy, I want a boy, not for a toy, but to annoy', and became bawdier with every line. During my research I was also given a photograph of VE day in 1945, at the centre of which is Lil, her arms linked with my grandmother Isabella. On reflection, not the most unusual of friendships.

* * *

On Sunday evenings in the summer, Mum, Dad and I would wander up Victoria Park Road to a pub where Lil would sing with Mum. The pub was populated by nancy boys and I would stand outside with my packet of crisps with the soggy salt in a twist of blue paper and watch the proceedings. To a man the nancies were dressed in suave suits, most wore trilby hats and make-up and one in particular was a beauty, nicknamed Chiquita, as he sang the song of that name. They would entertain the packed pub until closing time.

Unlike Maisie, Lil had no profession but had a string of menial jobs in the area. She cleaned pubs; goodness knows what the supposed ghost in the Nag's Head on Hackney

Road made of her. She'd served in the pie and mash shop also on Hackney Road. She also had two rather intriguing modes of employment. One, during the war, was pushing barrow loads of service uniforms from the factory where they were made, to another down the road that did buttonholing. The other was pushing a cart in Spitalfields' Fruit and Vegetable Market. I mention these because I am assured that she did these in full female regalia, something that would be foolhardy even in today's supposed climate of tolerance.

It seems that nobody minded for as long as she and Maisie stayed within the manor of Bethnal Green and the nearby part of Hackney into the Broadway Market and Victoria Park they were safe. Up West, where they ventured occasionally, was another world and one from which they would sometimes return beaten and bruised. It can't have been all honey in the East End, however, as Lil was known to carry a knife. It was only pulled, it was said, when inquisitive and overly friendly strangers wandered into the pubs which she frequented.

Her wardrobe was massive, full of garments of which she was rightly proud. Once a fire broke out in the flats in which she lived and Lil was seen throwing her frocks and shoes out of the window before surrendering herself to a perplexed fireman on a ladder. We kids loved both of them. They were kind, funny and always had time for you.

My last recollection of Lil was when, at the age of eighteen, I had a Christmas job in 1970 delivering post. I had a parcel for her and she invited me in for a cuppa. Maisie was not in evidence but Lil and I sat and chatted about love, life and the universe. She had a hacking cough and everything was stained with nicotine, especially her fingers and teeth, and she was not long for this world.

The old days of performing were long gone and she'd made a concession to age in wearing trouser suits. Her hair was now a shorter version of the peroxide curls she'd once displayed, but the diamante jewellery shone as brightly as ever. She and Maisie had parted company for reasons nobody knew, but photos of Maisie were on display everywhere. I nodded towards them. She answered with one of those indescribable shrugs, which carried a lifetime's worth of love and regret.

* * *

During my investigations into writing the musical about Lil nobody had a clue as to Maisie's fate and I had given up any hope of finding out what had happened to her. Then, in 2006, Carol got a job at an insurance company in the City of London. The facilities manager was an ex-Bethnal Green boy called Danny to whom she gave a copy of the book I had written about the area surrounding Columbia Road. Five minutes later he came over, the book opened to a section about Lil and Maisie. It was in this most unexpected of fashions I found the end to the cycle of their lives.

'Here, that Maisie was my uncle Georgie.'

Not much later I sat in a wine bar in the City with Danny's sister, Maisie's niece, Lesley. Danny wasn't present, he was still unable to cope with what had happened to his uncle.

'We'd not heard from Uncle Georgie which was strange. It was Christmas Eve and he usually came around to us. So

Dad went around to see him; it was back in the early 1980s and he had a flat on Old Ford Road. Dad couldn't get an answer but the small bathroom window was open so he came back and got me as I was small enough to climb in.'

She had opened the door and let her father into the place. They'd followed a red trail from the bedroom to the lounge, where Georgie knelt crouched on the floor naked, clutching a crimson sheet sodden with his own blood. His head had been bashed in. He was still alive, but died in the ambulance on the way to hospital. It seems that he had taken someone home who had robbed and beaten him.

Nobody has ever been found for the murder. As Lesley said, 'He was only a poof to the police. They didn't even bother to look.'

The East End was known for violence and inflexibility of attitudes, but if you were part of the tribe, you belonged. Maisie's death was tragic because, even though she'd only moved half a mile away from Columbia Road, she was no longer within the community with whom she'd grown up and where she was accepted. Strangely anonymous to her neighbours, she had been lying in the freezing cold for at least forty-eight hours before her family had found her.

I am pleased that Lil passed on before Maisie, because Maisie's end would have destroyed her. No matter that they argued constantly and were at loggerheads for much of their relationship, there had been huge affection there.

Chapter 5

The Dress Shop

The room was unkempt, untidy and in need of a paint. Nobody other than me seemed to notice that the ceiling was cracked and that rain seeped in around the window frame, or that from time to time mice would scurry across the floor. This was the workroom in the haberdasher's shop owned by my aunts; F. and L. Wilkinson, for Florrie and Lillie, at number 152 Columbia Road, immediately opposite my home.

On Saturday mornings women came in for fittings of the clothes they had ordered, and gossip flowed in an endless stream. It was reminiscent of the baths with the exception that they could see one another as they spoke. The stories were not as earthy as the ones I had absorbed in the steamy mists of York Hall; these women had enough money to spend on bespoke clothes so they carried at least a patina of class with them. Yet the tales were similar: personal, painful and oft-times bitchy. Most of them I didn't know, they were the wives of businessmen from the area or businesswomen themselves. The publican who ran the Blade Bone pub on Bethnal Green Road was a habitué of my aunts' establishment, where they attempted to create an elegance for her squat frame. She had the bandiest legs I have ever seen and her nose looked as if it had been broken several times. She was pugnacious in every way. I found her fascinating, and would walk behind her on the street trying to understand how she remained upright. All of this I observed when as a teenager I had a Saturday job serving in the shop at the front of the business. Then I was allowed to stand and watch the proceedings, the assumption being that I would become a dressmaker like the rest of the women in my family.

At age eight, though, I spent much of my time in the kitchen that sat behind the dress shop. It was a cold autumnal afternoon and an open fire warmed the small room, which like many others in my life had too much furniture. There was the obligatory dresser with attendant knick-knacks and photographs. Two armchairs (not matching) placed either side of the fireplace and a table and four chairs. Pride of place was a wall cabinet in which Lillie kept her best crockery and her 4711 cologne, the only perfume women seemed to wear in 1960. Its blue label was a dash of colour amid the gloom. Her husband, another George, sat with me at the table. It was covered with a cloth that had once been white, but too many food stains and rings from teacups had rendered it an unattractive shade of yellowy-grey.

We were playing a game called buttons. Living among dressmakers, buttons were in plentiful supply. The button tin sat between us, Uncle George sat on my right, as we matched up the types and colours, trying to get six of the same to win. It was a game of passing the time for him as he was babysitting me. The women in the family had gone out somewhere this particular day, and my father was at work.

He was bald; fronds of ginger hair sprouted in a semi-circle around the back of his head. I always remember him as brown and white. He had the whitest shiniest skin I have ever seen and he wore brown clothes at all times. George worked odd hours in the print in Fleet Street; he was a typesetter on one of the big dailies. He was also a drinker, and as we played his hands shook. He and Aunt Lillie were unable to have children; he would have been a good father, but some things are not meant to be. It became darker outside and rain began to fall. Almost the only light came from the fire. He stopped playing and stared at the flames. My arms began to tingle as a solid silence fell between us. The room was chill but he was sweating. I waited.

'I shouldn't tell you this . . .' He trailed off.

'I gave her a piece of chocolate and she died,' he began again.

And then he told me how he'd been part of the troops who had liberated Bergen-Belsen concentration camp in April 1945. I have no idea what sparked it. Why, in 1960, he should decide to relive and recount that awful scene and to me, but he did.

'We smelt it miles away. There we were all jolly thinking we'd just motor on to our destination and then be home soon, but instead we walked into hell.'

I knew what the Nazis had done, the newspapers were full of it when I was growing up, with attendant photographs. The Pathé News before the films that Dad took me to on Saturday afternoons often had features about hunts for war criminals, telling us what they were being sought for; but to hear it first hand was another thing altogether.

'They had eaten bits of one another, do you know that? How can you fathom that?'

I couldn't and neither could he, how could anybody who was sane? Holding my hand, he talked about bulldozing bodies into mass graves that held 5,000 at a time. Of making the German guards bury the typhus-infected bodies with their own hands.

'I couldn't look at their eyes as the corpses rolled into the pits, but these days it is all that I see when I close my eyes to sleep.'

But he couldn't sleep, except with drink, and as he got older it became more and more difficult to find oblivion.

He talked on, told me that there was no water in the camp, virtually no food and the women, for it was mostly women, had died of starvation.

'We had to fire on them to stop them raiding the food stores. My god, we should have just smashed them open and let them run riot, poor bastards.'

For a long while we sat in silence, our game unfinished on the cloth in front of us.

'Lin, I don't want you to talk about this. Don't even tell your mum.'

I said nothing. Eventually when it was almost pitch black outside he stood and put some fuel on the fire.

'I won't tell,' I said.

He smiled at me.

'Thank you.'

'Does Aunt Lillie know?'

He shook his head. It was obviously shared just between he and me.

'Glass of milk?'

Sometimes he would smile wistfully and wink, but neither of us mentioned it again. Over the years his shakes became worse and one day he had what they thought was a stroke. Like Clara before, his face was distorted, but he was compos mentis and unlike Clara he had some decent care. He was taken into the London Hospital. I took in a tennis ball for him to squeeze as the doctors had said it would help him regain the use of his right hand, which had become useless. Nothing helped, so they opened up his head to find a massive tumour which was inoperable, and he died. In the years since I have so often wished that I'd asked him why he told me, a child, but I never did.

The next summer I spent some of my holidays with Mum at the factory that she ran for Raphael on Pritchards Row. It was inordinately hot, and one day Rafe treated the factory to ice creams. I helped the tea lady Violet cut up the chunk in which it came and make wafer sandwiches for everybody. She was a short, portly woman with hair which was dyed a screaming black, if such a thing exists, and wore clothes and jewellery that teetered on the obscene. Her predilection was plunging necklines in which her bosoms bubbled and bounced and threatened to erupt into freedom. She wasn't happy at having her pristine tables awash with my attempts at cutting the ice cream into slices, but she bore it as it was the boss's wish.

Afterwards I sat on the cold concrete stairs, with Uncle Israel, and enjoyed the cold dribble as we sucked and chewed our way through the rapidly melting pleasure in our hands. Of course he was not my uncle, he was nobody's uncle. Mum had told me never to ask about the numbers on the arms of many of the people Rafe employed. I didn't know at the time that he sponsored survivors from the Nazi death camps to come and work in the UK. Israel noticed my guarded look at the fading blue script on his forearm. He hugged me to him; he was a big jaded bear of a man with white hair.

'Ah girlie,' he said, and like Uncle George told me his story. It was the tale like that of so many, for he was the sole survivor of an extended family. He was by now an old man and really could not work very well, but Rafe protected him from criticism of those who had not the wit to figure out why he was there.

He too died soon after, a blessed relief to him I imagine. It is for the likes of Israel that I hope there is a heaven, full of the family and the children he lost, all waiting for him to join them.

* * *

It is so far past midnight, that I daren't look at the clock. Carol is sleeping soundly, a soft snore escapes rhythmically from her mouth as I stare at the carpet in our lounge room. It is a fine Wilton, but belongs on the floor of a pub – its reds, oranges and yellows would truly hide any stain. Even by the dim light shed through the window by the lamp outside, it is hideous. Last night Carol had asked me why we were here in this grotty run-down part of town.

My rationale for returning to the East End hasn't so much haunted as bemused me. I am a scientist after all and should be all logic and straight-line thinking. Empiricism is the order of the day. Encounter a problem, examine it, test it and resolve it. Perform the experiment. But memories don't come neatly packaged to be selected, analysed or dissected. There is nothing clinical about life, nothing clean, logical or well ordered. Life is a form of chaos which surely the memories that assail me prove.

Mother always viewed life as a fight, each day was a mountain to climb, a struggle to survive, and she imbued this into me as sternly as she could. 'If you can put your feet on the floor and get out of bed, you're doing all right' was a mantra that she lived by. I think of her struggling with my precocity amid a life in which she hardly had time to take a breath for herself. As I age I wonder more and more at the energy she had for others and seldom for herself.

* * *

Her home schooling of me had meant that I was far ahead of the reading age at Columbia Primary and hence had rapidly consumed most of the books they had on offer. There were few books at home either, so I joined the local library that lay buried within the 1950s splendour of the Dorset Estate flats. It was a completely circular building which sat like a grey concrete pod amid the tower blocks that surrounded it. There were high-level windows all around making it light and pleasant on all but the darkest of winter days. I was aware of it because my aunts went there to borrow the potboilers with which they whiled away their leisure hours. Derring-do novels about eighteenth-century pirates were a favourite, especially the Poldark series.

On the day I first went in, the librarian tutted in a most audible fashion. Almost nine years old and without an adult and I wanted to enter her sanctuary; it wasn't right. She peered down at me over the counter as I stood on tiptoe to hand in the joining slip on which I had forged Mum's signature. I'm sure that she would have signed it, but this was something I wanted to do for myself. Miss Librarian shooed me around the counter into the children's section and kept an eagle eye on me as I pulled out tomes and examined them.

She was a thin, taut woman with severe spectacles who wore an air of martyrdom. I didn't wonder until much later if a posting to Bethnal Green was like one to the Gobi Desert. It was in those days a no man's land for foreigners; anyone not from the East End that was. During the years of our association she learned to tolerate me; eventually even my forays into the adult sections of English fiction no longer raised a sigh. She even allowed my cousin David, three years younger than me, entry into her world. He was equally precocious and he loved mathematics. We would spend many a happy hour during school holidays hiding away from the gangs from the local area who loved terrorising the likes of us. Whatever was happening at home, or on the street, I could disappear into my world of books.

My time at Columbia Primary was coming to an end. I'd been a pupil since the age of three and had been in the top class for two years, as there was no mechanism for taking the eleven-plus early. The form teacher, who managed to teach forty pupils in three streams, was a force of nature. Mrs Holmes had pure white curly hair and seemed ancient. She did retire soon after I left, so I suppose that in 1963 she was in her late fifties. She was calm in any storm that came her way. Snails being let loose and crawling up walls never fazed her. Major fights and fisticuffs were met by a caning or a wallop around the head with *Aesop's Fables*.

Even so, despite her best efforts, I was easily bored and spent a fair few hours standing in the corner observing the ceiling. Yet she was kind and understanding, and gave me homework as she felt I should go to Central Foundations Girls' School (CFGS), which was a grammar school in the City of London.

I struggled with maths, but I could read easily so ignored studying the English exercises that she set for me. Assumption is the source of many a disappointment, as I failed my English eleven-plus but much to my surprise passed the maths. One of my cousins went to the local secondary modern school, St Jude's, and there was talk of me going there, but I was obsessed with going to CFGS and deeply upset when it looked as if that wouldn't happen. By now my reading had opened up other worlds to me and I wanted to be part of those, wanted to lead a different kind of life, and by repute the school was the pathway to that.

Already by age eleven I had no predilection to marry. Home life wasn't poor. I knew of girls being abused by their fathers or brothers or treated as skivvies, and there was none of that. Yet, what I saw didn't entice me to follow my parents' lead. It seemed a hard, repetitive life, and it was.

My youthful self failed to appreciate that only by relying on routine could my mother make it from one end of the week to the next. Dad was the archetypal man of his time and, although Mum always earned a greater salary than he, his contribution to the home was purely his wages. He would come in from work and sit until his dinner was put in front of him. He never washed up, shopped or contributed in any way to the running of the home. His stubborn refusal to move to a more modern house, or even upgrade ours to a level of some comfort, grated. Once, when I was trying to have a conversation with him, to be confronted with the wall of the *Daily Mirror*, I reached for his matches and set the newspaper alight. I did get his attention that time, particularly as the fire singed his abundant eyebrows.

When the letter came inviting Mum and me to an interview at CFGS I was elated, but I seemed to be the only one. There was a pervasive sense of dread at home. This was the 'posh' school and some kind of inverted snobbery seemed to envelope the very idea of it. Tony, who by now was a City and Guilds qualified engineer, began to call me 'Princess', and Mum continually warned me not to be disappointed when I failed to get in. Dad remained silent but did smile at the news, which I took as positive, if passive, encouragement. On reflection it was all very odd. Two of my elder cousins were at grammar schools and a couple of girls on Columbia Road went to CFGS, so I wondered why I was being warned off.

The day of the interview dawned. It was warm and sunny and Mum took the afternoon off work to take me along. That first time we got the bus up to Bishopsgate and walked through Spitalfields Market, where the school was situated. The whole area stank, rotting fruit and veg lay in the August sunshine waiting for the rubbish men to clean up. The stench of cabbage gently being cooked by the sun's rays is something that is hard to forget.

We walked across a small forecourt, up a few stairs and entered via a set of heavy wooden doors. Inside was a small waiting area outside of the headmistress's office. The walls were adorned with lists of head girls and former notables written in gold on oak boards. Seamlessly, a secretary appeared and asked us to sit on one of the bench seats and wait. It was 3 p.m. and the sun was slanting through the fanlight above the doors, illuminating the marble floor and us with a warm glow. It was quiet, calm, and I felt as I did when I lost myself in a good book, as if I were in a timeless space. After a quarter of an hour or so Mum began one of her warnings about expectations, just as another mother and daughter team emerged rather tearfully from an office door and scuttled out of the building.

Of course, all of the clever girls who had flown through their eleven-plus had been enrolled; I was part of the B team, those also-rans who might be allowed to enter the hallowed gates. My stomach did a somersault. We heard a door open and a voice call out my name.

The headmistress at my primary school, Miss Abbott, was short, squat and ancient. She wielded the cane with aplomb and bustled around like a queen bee. Nothing to date in my life had prepared me for Elaine Dunford. Later I got to know her room very well, but of that day all I can recall is the large polished wooden desk behind which she sat, and Elaine herself. My mother wore the top fashions, there were some bunts to be had in the rag trade, but Elaine was elegance personified on another scale. And she was beautiful. I'd never heard a voice like it, low, melodious and kind. She wore something scarlet, red was her favourite colour, and a soft scent permeated the air.

She indicated that we sit. At age thirty-seven, she was one of the youngest heads in the country. She wasted no time in getting to the point.

'So Linda, why do you think you failed your English?'

'She's a worrier, my Lin,' Mum interjected.

Elaine smiled and nodded at me to speak.

'I just did my arithmetic homework.'

'From Mrs Holmes?'

The penny dropped with Mum as to who was to blame for this meeting as I nodded.

'You did very well at it.'

Mum butted in. 'Listen Mrs . . .'

'Dunford.'

'Dunford. We're not wanting her to be worried. She's a strange child.'

I could have kicked her; I didn't.

Elaine breathed in and gently flared her nostrils.

'In what way Mrs Wilkinson?'

Mum spoke of my being a 'watcher', as she called me, and a worrier. She even mentioned my obsession with Clara, hinting that I needed protecting from the world rather than taking part in it. It was like being back in the cretin phase they had assumed that I was as a young child. I was furious; I think it showed.

'Mrs Wilkinson, would you mind awfully waiting outside?'

There was a long pause.

'Please.'

She didn't like it, Mum, I doubt if I would have, but she left.

'So, you ignored the English for the maths?'

I nodded and began to speak. I spoke as I had never spoken before about what I had read, what I liked, the library that I went to, proving my credentials.

'Is your mother right to worry? It is a tough school, have no doubts about that.'

'I want to learn.'

She asked me about home life, my brother, my parents' professions, all the time glancing at the paper in front of her.

'Easily bored, Mrs Holmes says. Are you?'

I nodded.

'And you want?'

I was confused.

'In life.'

It's a big question for a child, for anybody.

'Not to be bored, I suppose,' was the best I could come up with.

She smiled broadly. 'Yes, something that unites all of us.'

'Did anyone help you at home, with your maths?'

'Dad.'

He had. For some reason he had put down the *Daily Mirror*, got out his books from the war when he'd been trained as an aircraft engineer and guided me through the exercises.

'He is happy for you to come here?'

Should I lie? I lied.

'He'd be very happy.'

'But Mum taught me to read, when I was three.' She was my mum after all.

I saw an eyebrow raise. As an educator she had to ask how. I could tell that she was intrigued. The tale of the shells surprised her. She then asked about any other influences on my life; I told her about Nan and her stories and how the clouds reminded you of people. I left out the laudanum, it seemed best.

Mum was silent on the bus ride home. Dad smiled broadly when I told him that I was going to be a grammar school girl. Mum put his dinner in front of him that night with the phrase, 'So how are we going to pay for it?'

The 'it' was the uniform.

I was fat then and have always been large. This was important, because the school blazer had to be made for me. It could not come off the peg. Gamages department store stood at Holborn Circus. It was old, stuffy and expensive. I could feel the spleen rising in mother as the price for the garment was quoted, and I can equally recall her eyeing some bottle-green woollen fabric with which she could have easily made the blazer. She was used to making everything I wore.

'But, madam, the school insignias are individually embroidered onto the jacket.'

This was pure bunk of course and in the end I had the same badge on every subsequent jacket that Mother made. She was a demon at unpicking.

All in all, she did quite well; true the emerald, rather

than bottle-green, jumper didn't pass muster and the cheap gingham check fabric she bought from a stall down the Roman Road market ran when washed, but other than that I was almost bespoke Wilkinson throughout my stay. A few things she couldn't make, like the ghastly bottle-green knickers we had to wear for gym, and the gym tunics themselves, and the lab coats of which I got through aplenty.

Over the preceding couple of years I had developed a friendship with some kids who lived in the Peabody Estate flats on Shipton Street, which lies behind Columbia Road. I'd go and play at their home and they at mine, but as most kids did we spent most of our life on the streets. Peabody flats had a large tarmac playground area which was car-free and, although there weren't many vehicles in those days, this was a good place to kick a football or run around without fear of injury or causing damage to someone's property.

I'd principally made friends with a girl called June. She had a younger brother and they lived in a first floor flat. She was about my age and it was nice to have a girl to play with. I was excited about my new school, but when I told her about CFGS her response had been odd, chilly even, but I took no notice.

The next time I went to call for her, she was in the playground and showed no signs of letting me up to her flat. No matter, we occupied ourselves with hopscotch. Shortly afterwards her brother came down with an open tin of house paint with sticks in it with which they proceeded to daub my clothes. Their mother and father stood with crossed arms and sour expressions, looking down from their balcony as their offspring assaulted me in the forecourt below. I was chased from the estate and ran home crying.

I had been wearing a new coat which Mum had made for me and it was ruined. She stormed around there demanding an explanation. They didn't want the likes of me playing with their kids. They didn't like snobs and posh gits and I was never to show my face again.

Mum never said 'I told you so', but even if she had I knew where I was better off. I retreated into the world of books.

Chapter 6

Grammar School

Before I went to CFGS I was allowed to spend one final afternoon with Nan and for some reason my mother insisted that I wear my new school uniform. It was the first time I had worn the blessed blazer outside and I prayed that June and her brother were occupied elsewhere and wouldn't spot me. I had been shaken by being attacked, but Mum in her fashion had sat me down and put it in perspective.

'It's them that has the problem,' she'd said. 'Not you.'

'I don't understand.'

'It's called jealousy, love.'

'But June didn't want to go to my school.' I was just about holding back my tears.

'There's none as queer as folk, that you will learn. Go on Lin, go see Nan, you'll be fine.'

Nan had been increasingly unwell and hadn't been out of her flat for over a year. I let myself into the flat and entered her bedroom. Bejewelled and powdered she lay propped on pillows, as it transpired just a whisper away from death.

'What you wearing that for?'

'Mum said I should, said you'd like to see it.'

'It's Spitalfields' uniform?'

I nodded.

'Grammar school. Maybe your mother was right to take you away from me and the pub.'

I helped her on with the oxygen mask that was keeping her alive while she fumbled in her handbag for a crumpled ten-shilling note. 'Here,' she said, 'take this, for being clever.'

We sat in silence as she gulped air into what remained of her lungs. The great pools of her green eyes wrinkled with amusement. 'What are you going to do with it, learning?'

There it was, the question that nobody had to date had the courage, or forethought, to ask of me. I wanted to escape the smelly stairwells like the one outside Nan's flat. Escape a house with an outside toilet, no heating, no hot water. Lose an accent as thick as treacle. I wanted to be out there in what was to me the real world, full of other smells, other experiences.

'Don't you shrug at me. I know what you're thinking.'

'What?'

'You want to run away, will run away, but you'll most likely come back one day.'

'Why should I?'

'Because we're real.'

'Other people are real.'

'Not in the same way. I've met them, afraid anaemic scallywags. Not like you, you've got fight.'

She paused, measuring her words.

'I don't want for you what me and your mother had. No, I don't mean that. You'll learn lots from books, you must, but there's a bit of you that will always be here, even when you don't know it. It'll sneak up on you one day.'

I had a fleeting vision of the white scudding clouds we had sat and observed those few years ago. For a moment companionable silence reigned.

'Besides, just 'cause you'll see more people don't mean you'll see more,' she continued warming to her theme.

'What?'

'We all has the same experiences love, with or without money. With or without learning. We're all born, live and die. If you're lucky someone might love you and you them. If not, it's all the same.'

She coughed painfully, holding her chest, trying to contain the agony. Finally, gasping, she lay back, the mask all askew, I turned off the air.

'Got any gin, Nan?'

Her smile was as broad as ever: 'Thanks love, make sure you pep it up right, now.'

I did, melding the syrup lovingly as I had been taught, and we sat sharing one last afternoon of colours and crystal light courtesy of that squat brown bottle. It was a bright and beautiful afternoon and the tree outside her bedroom window glowed hard with new greenery. Her once powerful frame was shrunken into the bed, white on white, the only colours a slash of red for her lips and, as always, her eyes, which in that final laudanum haze challenged even the leaves for their splendour.

The sun had long left the room when I stood to take my leave. She lay more deeply now, almost buried, a wizened shadowed reflection of a life hard lived. It was the last time I would kiss her still soft cheek, and smell the orris root face powder warmed by her flesh.

'Bye Nan.'

'Bye love, look after yourself.'

As I turned to close the door she was already asleep, her breathing uneven and shallow, enlivened by a gentle snoring. It was in the soft grey light of that early evening I said goodbye to my best friend.

The school building was neither beautiful nor welcoming. Long marble-floored corridors and high ceilings gave it the feel of an institution more in tune with illness than education. Two wide staircases led to the first and the second floors, where the majority of school life was played out. Rather like servants' quarters in stately homes, there was another precipitous stairway at the top of one side of the building that led further upwards into the eaves. Here, a series of small rooms for study vied for space with broken equipment and old wicker boxes full of clothes from school plays. Derelict blackboards, the last lesson still scrawled upon them, lay next to their defunct easels in corners by fireplaces which had not been lit in years. The central heating seldom reached the radiators here, making the spaces difficult to use in the winter, and so they became the refuge of smokers and the nervous who needed time for themselves.

The first floor housed the science laboratories and the museum in which were displayed the relics found when subterranean renovations had taken place. Alongside this was an eclectic mix of memorabilia garnered on visits to places as exotic as Mesopotamia and Japan by staff and pupils alike. Queuing up for physics lessons I had ample time to admire a small glass vial from AD 200 found beneath the toilets when they had been rebuilt in the 1930s. In my fifth year at school an unsuspecting plumber while investigating a blocked pipe in the basement had found a skull. In shock he'd fled from the building. Mr Reeve, the caretaker, ran after him, skull in hand while calling out.

'Stop, don't worry, it'll be Roman.'

He was right, the school lay just outside of the north gate of Londinium and was built over a Roman burial site. 'Fred', the Roman skull, was popped into the exhibits cabinet and had been a feature of school life thenceforward. In 1999 a lead coffin in which lay a woman of high caste was discovered on the site of the school. It caused much excitement among academics and laymen alike. Those of us who'd attended CFGS weren't surprised at all.

The second floor housed the arts space and humanities classrooms. Form classrooms were bunched at the two ends of the building and, as you progressed through the school, you moved upwards and outwards, from the dark of the ground floor up into the light.

'Omnipresent', 'dominant' and 'all pervasive' were terms that I heard used to describe Elaine Dunford, usually by those mistresses who were not her natural allies. These teachers, unable to take the pace, or what was demanded of them, would come and go. As much as her crusade was to modernise the school, Elaine relied upon a solid base of older females to instruct and inspire in us a passion for learning. As a teacher herself she was mesmeric, commanding total respect by the sheer acuteness of her presence. She focused on two subjects: her own which was English, the other film appreciation.

With English Literature she was clear and precise, sometimes stern if you failed to catch on as quickly as she would have hoped, but she was always fair in her criticism. Her love of Chaucer and Shakespeare were equalled in every way by authors who sat well with her feminist and humanist leanings. She shared some of these books with the school at assemblies. These daily gatherings were a mixture of religion, to which she gave a nod, and progressive thought. A favourite was *Perelandra* by C.S. Lewis. Ostensibly part of a science fiction trilogy, it imagines a world in which the Fall of Adam and Eve from grace did not happen. Based on Milton's *Paradise Lost* it is a breathtaking reimagining of a world in which nothing is as it seems. His evocation of transcendental sexuality, in which he describes a fluidity which is neither male nor female, is fascinating.

At the other end of the spectrum was Betty Friedan's 1963 masterpiece *The Feminine Mystique*, from which Elaine read extracts with great relish. Fearlessly she would voice Friedan's take on the place and plight of women at every level of society. My skin would light up on these occasions, for although the older teachers were doyens of their fields, blatant feminism made some of them uncomfortable. I could sense their squirming and almost feel the redness of their cheeks.

Elaine performed a high-wire balancing act on many levels. As I got to know both her and the school I saw that someone with true vision had given her the job. Her vice headmistress, a Miss Iddisson, was older and rigid. I don't think that she was particularly popular with even her peers and I have often wondered if it was she who had been the next in line for promotion, only to be usurped by the glamorous creature who now stood on the dais channelling Freidan and telling us that, 'No woman gets an orgasm from shining the kitchen floor.'

Standing there so formally, with hair coiffured and wearing her headmistress's gown, I could not imagine her with her head thrown back in the throes of passion any more than I could have imagined her stolid deputy doing the same.

In film appreciation, another person glimpsed out from the confines that the job imposed. I imagine that she must have instigated the subject as part of the curriculum as she took such joy in teaching it. We would hunker down in a small corner classroom on the ground floor, which was used because it had only one window. A blackout curtain would be pulled and for some reason we sat on the desks to view the film. Elaine would sit next to the projector in a similar fashion, hug her knees, and begin her dissection of the piece at hand. In the dark, with the pressure to perform removed she relaxed, her voice softened, and it felt as if she were one of us.

The first film we saw was *Battleship Potemkin*. The famous Odessa steps sequence was dissected from the screaming woman's point of view. We created a whole life for both the woman and a back story for the scene which in our hands delved far into the past.

The mixture of movies studied was eclectic. *Some Like It Hot* was shown for light relief but we saw a lot of Hitchcock, particularly *The Birds* and *Marnie*. The film I recall that had a real resonance for me, and the only British film and the only film about working-class life we viewed, was Shelagh

Delaney's *A Taste of Honey*. There were many other British films she may have chosen, but this was contemporary and dealt with the issues of racism, homosexuality, alcoholism and pregnancy outside of marriage. It also brutally exposed a failed mother for what she was.

Elaine's whole *raison d'être* as both a teacher and a human being was to gently push us towards liberating our minds and thus ourselves from accepted concepts of womanhood and our roles within society. Such was her appearance and demeanour that one would have imagined her being presented at a royal debutante's ball, and yes she'd had a privileged upbringing in Manchester. So how did she come to be fighting so strongly for a bright but underprivileged set of girls from the slums of the East End? It's a question that remains unanswered. Time and time again she went out on a limb to protect her girls. I thought that I had dreamt that she arranged abortions for pupils. I remembered girls developing very obvious bumps and returning after a few days minus them, with nothing being said. At a recent reunion I found out that it was true.

At her funeral in 2015 I met some women who as pupils had gone to live with her when their home life had become too 'difficult'. She had taken pupils on holiday, subbed their mums out when money was tight and in retrospect probably broke every rule in the book.

Like many, I was both in awe of her and loved her. She is the reason that I sit and write this book today; she told me that I could do anything if I put my mind to it.

Yet she was not universally loved. She could be terse and distant. If you showed promise but balked at a hurdle, or simply did not try, she had no time for you. Success as measured in examination passes wasn't her game, she wanted you to believe in yourself and have fight.

'It's hard out there,' she said. 'You have to be ready for it.'

Pupils came and went. Grammar schools aren't an ossified club for a static elite. We had a stream of girls over the years that entered the school late, or gave up if the going was too hard.

After my incident with the paint smearing by June and her brother I was bereft of local friends. Only one other girl from Columbia Primary School went to CFGS, Denise. I hadn't been close to her as she lived a few streets away in a block of flats. The East End was a set of small tribal villages with their own codes of behaviour, and her bush telegraph and ours did not intersect. We recognised one another on the first day and got into the habit of walking to school together. She was gossamer thin with pale hair and skin, which rendered her almost translucent. Whereas I struggled with the collar of my shirt, which was always too tight, hers hung around her like a noose. She looked, and was, a sensitive, almost otherworldly person.

We would walk down Brick Lane with its Jewish beigel shops and grocers, through the detritus of the fruit and vegetable market and into school. I wasn't an exceptional pupil but I was engaged and enthused and would babble away about school, filling a silence between us which otherwise became oppressive.

After two years, Denise disappeared. One day I called for her to be told she was ill and she never returned to CFGS.

'She has a nervous disorder, Linda dear,' Elaine told me when I asked her what had happened.

I sat opposite her in her office, taking in the scent from a vase of lilies which sat nearby.

'It can come on with the advent of menstruation,' she said, citing a catchall, but probably accurate, rationale for Denise's absence.

'She didn't like it here,' I said. 'It was all too difficult.'

'What in particular?'

'Latin mostly, she liked maths though.'

'And you? Do you find them easy, or difficult?'

I didn't like either subject, but I wasn't game to tell her as I knew I'd get extra tuition, which on top of eight periods a day I wouldn't relish.

'I'm fine.'

'And your parents, how are they?'

'All right.'

'My door is always open.'

She knew that Mum and Dad had only been to one parents' evening. It hurt me at first that they never attended another. Finally, I simply stopped giving them the slip of paper informing them of the date.

They'd both felt out of their depth; or at least that's what I guessed, as we never discussed it.

Although I wasn't particularly impressed by my progress, I had tried to stick to Mother's demand that I stay within the top three of my class. I managed that pretty well, except for the aforementioned Latin and maths, and it was Mrs Gray who I think had terrified the life out of Mum and Dad with her insistence that Latin lay at the heart of all civilisation.

She was enough to put anyone off when she was in full classics mode. My parents cared about me, but school life was my own. If my annual report showed me slipping, Dad would take me aside and ask if anything was wrong, but aside from that it was my domain. From time to time I bored them rigid with something that interested me, like translating the Latin on headstones in churchyards, which was a fad I had for a while and the only part of the language at which I excelled. Then while I was doing my A levels I became obsessed about the tectonic plate theory of the development of the earth and the evolution of volcanoes; I loved studying volcanoes. But there were things aplenty my parents would not have wanted to know about.

As headmistress, it transpired that Elaine had more than just her 480 pupils to worry about.

'Vaginismus, girls, is a dreadful condition.'

Miss Holt, our history teacher, had not only the remarkable ability to bring the Punic Wars to life, she would also spontaneously interject moments from her own life into our lessons. We were in the third form when this joyous piece of information was shared with us. I was seated at the back of the class sitting next to the other W., Elaine Wilson, E.W.

'What's that?'

E.W. shrugged a 'don't know'. Onward ploughed Miss Holt as we put down our pens and listened to her recount her adventures of the previous evening. If my memory serves me correctly, the penis in question belonged to a man called Hugh, whom Miss H. had known for a goodly while. She'd had the affliction before she said, but Hugh was supremely unimpressed by it and had left her alone and frustrated to seek solace elsewhere.

Then a switch went on and, as if nothing had happened, we were back in 218 BC with Hannibal and his three-dozen elephants traversing the Alps. Pens at the ready once more, the history lesson coasted to its usual conclusion with notes on what to read up on before the next session.

Miss Holt disappeared for a while; we were told that she suffered from 'nerves'. When she returned, she was much quieter and I suspect sedated, but her lessons never lost their spark. She wandered off-piste from time to time, albeit not so controversially as on that day, which had seen me scurry to the dictionary to understand exactly what she had been talking about. I note this event because it showed both her frailty and courage. What she felt when she came back to face us one can only guess, but return she did. We were not the kindest of people when the herd mentality took hold, but we sensed her fragility and left well alone.

Not that there was any commonality in the illness or disorder which afflicted them, but Miss Holt's outburst and her subsequent disappearance had reminded me of Clara, who was still alive but living in an institution. Finally, the authorities had become involved in her care and she had gone away the spring before I had come to the school. Since then she had been all but eradicated from our lives.

As a consequence of her leaving, I had my own bedroom. It had been my brother's; he now inhabited Alice's old kitchen and scullery. Alice resided in the front bedroom, which was next to mine. We only spoke when we had to and it had been that way since long before Clara had been removed. One night I drifted upward out of sleep to the smell of burning. It was coming from her room. I went in. She'd knocked the shade of a lamp onto the bulb, the fabric was partly plastic and it was smoking. Sitting in Clara's old armchair she looked up at my approach, and as I turned off the light we stared at one another.

She grabbed my arm and pushed me onto a stool at her feet, in her lap were the war medals that every poor blighter who died in the First World War had been awarded. She had several of them.

'I was thirty-four when your grandfather died,' she said, holding a medal up towards me.

'A medal and a letter, couldn't eat that, could we?'

Was it a tacit acknowledgment that she knew that to me she had become a monster, or a plea for me to understand her life? I recall her rambling on and telling me about each of the men the medals named; it shocked me as I'd had no idea how many of my family had perished in that indescribable conflict. In the end, her tears spent, I helped her into bed. She was almost bent double with arthritis and her knees were a swollen mess of effusions.

She died not long afterwards. Cousin David and I had gone to visit her at Bethnal Green Hospital; it was expected of us as dutiful grandchildren and there seemed little point in not complying. At the entrance was a pentagonal wooden booth with a viewing grille in which sat the duty porter who would direct you to the correct ward. He flipped through the list towards the end of the alphabet. 'Mrs Wilkinson?'

'Our nan.'

He looked from David to me and back.

'You know she was very sick? And old? I'm sorry love, she's gone.'

David didn't quite hear so was surprised when I turned on my heel and walked out onto Cambridge Heath Road.

'She's dead,' I told him.

I was fourteen years old and my grandmother Alice had just died. When I got home I cried, but they were tears of relief not regret.

We now had more space at home than we could ever have dreamed of. In 1966 Tony had married and bought his own house in Dagenham. His room was as he had left it, ready for his occasional visits, except that Mum now instated her sewing machine there. My parents occupied Alice's old bedroom and their former bedroom was knocked through into the lounge to make a dining and living space. No thought, however, was given to providing a bathroom or inside toilet.

With the house to ourselves I found that my studies began to go really well. Relieved of all that Alice's presence had meant to me I felt free for the first time. The leaden miasma that she had carried with her was no more and the inner tension which had categorised my life dissipated.

The running sore that was Clara was still present, but at a remove which could be handled. Maturity was approaching but it would take almost a lifetime to unravel the conflicting emotions that I felt about my family in her regard.

Chapter 7

Head Girl

Elaine and I had consumed more brandy than we should have. As I was seventeen it hadn't surprised me that she had offered me a drink to assuage the dreadful colds we both had.

It was December 1969 and we were about to take part in the annual carol service at our Church of St Botolph without Bishopsgate. This was a highlight of the school calendar, involving all the pomp and circumstance that the City of London could offer a school such as ours. We were allied to the Worshipful Company of Fan Makers and they would be in attendance in full regalia, with silver fans atop mahogany poles.

I had sneezed my way indelicately into her room and collapsed onto a chair. I was head girl and school soloist and my throat felt like a desert. Since my elevation I had become used both to her room and her. We'd had a rocky start when I'd spent the book money I'd been awarded for being elected on boots and a handbag; she must have wondered how the year would go, but somehow we'd navigated the blips and were now friends. I was her deputy in every way, she'd told me, and I had learned to take that seriously. I looked at her running eyes and a nose which would have done Rudolph the reindeer proud.

'I can't sing,' I said.

'And I can't speak,' she croaked.

The brandy seemed like a godsend, except that she shouldn't have drunk it, or maybe she should have.

We had ample time to talk and talk we did. I'd noticed an increasing sadness about her over the past months and a tendency to be more distant than usual. My skin had told me that all was not well, but I hadn't felt it my business to ask. I had wondered if the gossip that she was involved with the pottery teacher, Emmanuel Cooper, was correct. Having grown up with Diamond Lil, et al., I had put him in the 'Friend of Dorothy' box, which it transpired was true.

Slowly and haltingly she told me that her marriage was on the rocks. They could not have children of their own and this weighed heavily upon them. She desired nothing more than being a mother herself. Moreover, she was a woman outside of her time. She was a feminist almost before the word was invented, a free spirit who used the establishment to further her desires both for herself and us. It appeared that she and he no longer had a basis for a relationship. Divorce was still a difficult voyage to embark upon, but she acknowledged that was what she was going to have to do.

'You have to fight for yourself,' I remember saying. 'The way you fight for us.'

Her tears welled over and we indulged in another libation to womanhood.

I was used to drinking sherry; my father had taken me to The Perseverance pub and introduced me to it when I was twelve years old. Not that I couldn't have drank some at home, but he had wanted to take me out and show his girl off. Mother had been enraged as Dad and I seemed to have the same lack of understanding of moderation. Now into the jolly phase of drunkenness, Elaine and I agreed that I would sing superbly and she would read as well as she ever had. We had the one small problem, that of walking to the church, which was along the main road a few hundred yards away beyond Liverpool Street Station. Luckily Miss Iddisson, who at first tried to dissuade us from going to the service, bundled us giggling into a taxi. She sat opposite us as we tried to act like adults but failed abysmally at her stern expression.

I was in her seriously bad books already for, at an event earlier in the year, I had been dispensing warm blackcurrant cordial from an urn in the church hall only to have the tap come off in my hand. Not being able to keep up with the deluge it had gushed all over the floor. Not my fault, but she didn't view life that way.

We emerged from the taxi in a haze of alcohol fumes to enter a packed church. I went to the head of the choir, Elaine to the front just behind the Fan Makers. 'Once in Royal David's City' was struck up by the organ, and as we processed I opened my mouth and miraculously a sound came out. Elaine fared a little worse as she lost her place in her reading, but a judicious sneeze in December is acceptable behaviour to cover a boozy blunder.

Elaine regarded me as someone more mature than my age, which in many ways I was. Having grown up in adult company I had a patina of sophistication which I was able to use when required. However, I didn't have the experience to back it up.

My life outside of school was my parents, with whom I spent much of my spare time. We went to the theatre, the occasional restaurant and the few pubs that Mum would patronise. She and I still visited the street markets that were such a feature of the East End, but I had no life of my own. I made a few friends at school but I never socialised as others did. We never had the spare cash for me to go on the school trips abroad, which having heard about the rusting hulks of the ships used I wasn't bothered by. Any trips I had been on had been associated with the three subjects I had chosen for my A levels, botany, geography and zoology.

My passage through school had seen me veer towards science. I had no antipathy towards other subjects, but what I saw as the logical simplicity of these disciplines was attractive. That, coupled with some exceptional teaching, set me on a path which, minor detours aside, I followed until my mid-forties. Miss Holt's eccentricity in our history lessons was both equalled and surpassed by several of the mistresses who taught me, and for that I am profoundly grateful. I had toyed with studying physics, but I realised that the attraction of the subject was the fact that Mrs Hawkins, who taught it, was accident prone. Her lessons were explosive, literally, and in those pre-health and safety days we learned to shout 'duck' in time to avoid flying shrapnel from expansion of gases experiments which had gone wrong. We played with mercury on the bench, rolling it around with fascination. I wonder that none of us were poisoned. No, my metiers by the age of sixteen were to be biology and geography.

A Miss Jenkins taught biology. I had seen her around, of course. In the winter she sported a Barbour raincoat and a yellow rain hat, the type of which trawler men wore. She strode the streets with the aid of a gnarled wooden walking stick with which I had no doubt she cleared the pavement of other lesser beings. Her indoor couture consisted of a tweed skirt suit with waistcoat and brogue shoes. She wore lisle stockings, like those which I sold to the older ladies in my aunt's shop to hide varicose veins and other age-related blemishes.

At our first session with her she had swept her eyes across us seeking out the winners and losers. Small shrewish blue eyes twinkled behind pebble thick glasses; these were complemented by the voice of a well-modulated foghorn as she barked out the register. I had no doubt that her sexuality was other. She lived on the south coast with her brother and that was the sum of personal knowledge she shared with us. That and the fact that she was part of a breeding experiment to produce talented offspring conducted by the Huxley and Darwin families. There is no evidence to support this, but it may well have been true. Against all of the other teachers, this elderly, squat woman with a mannish haircut was the truest of bohemians.

Her laboratory, populated by plants of all shapes and sizes, was on the bright side of the school. It was in the first-floor corner and had tall windows on two sides. Standing on the dais in front of the blackboard she endlessly tossed the chalk in the air as she spoke of breeding experiments, of Gregor Mendel the monk who showed sex-linked genetics for the first time. 'The next time you see *Pisum sativum*, the garden pea, acknowledge its place in the history of science.'

Had she travelled to the exotic places she spoke of? I doubt it, yet her lectures were journeys through the dark underbelly of rainforests or up to the summits of mountains. *The Voyage of the Beagle* could have happened yesterday and you could almost hear the snap of rigging and feel the spray of the sea as she spoke of it. Investigators of the past came to life and I fell in love with her version of science and storytelling in equal measure. Her mind couldn't have been brighter, crisper or her attitudes more irreverent. Listening to her, I sometimes found myself thinking about the conversation that I'd had with my grandmother as she lay dying, about the school taking me away from my roots. Here was a woman whose roots seemingly resided in her intellect, which she carried everywhere. She had a bugbear about mediocrity, she could not abide it and if she thought your work was in that category she had no compunction in telling you. Unlike Elaine, who would try and get to the bottom of what was bothering you, life to Miss Jenkins was a battle to be won. Had I believed in reincarnation she would have been Wellington pushing his troops to victory without a thought for collateral damage.

Geography was taught in another way altogether. Mrs Porter was a bright young thing. Not one of Noël Coward's, but of the 1960s. Her faith in communism was profound and her belief in women's liberation as strong as Elaine's, but expressed differently. She would have been a decade younger than the headmistress and she occupied that part of the teacher's common room which was littered with overfull ashtrays, cups of half-drunk tea and with a peek here and there of underwear on the shelves probably which had been shed when changing to go on a night out.

The few times that I had cause to enter that room it made me think of trench warfare. It was elongated, running parallel to a corridor, and was reached by a steep set of stairs. The door opened centrally to the trench, as I saw it. The converse side to that occupied by the younger teachers was that of the older. Here everything was filed, folded and regimented. No space or place for frivolity. No posters announcing the next meeting of political parties adorned their walls, here operas and literature conferences were announced and the only thing that might spill over a shelf was some knitting. The Second World War had produced a hiatus in staffing and the gap between the two sides encompassed the time between the Edwardian and current eras. How I would have loved to have been a fly on one of those walls when conversations took place.

Like Miss Holt, Mrs Porter interjected her geography classes with details of her own life. Sex did appear on the smorgasbord, but more often it was politics which galvanised her. She was active in the anti-Vietnam War movement as it evolved. Alongside some other mistresses she took part in the 1968 riots in Paris. On 6 May the teachers unions of France had marched alongside the students to protest against the state closure of the Sorbonne. There had been much violence on both sides. Barricades were erected, tear gas was thrown and finally mounted police had attacked the protesters with baton charges. It was one of the first of such riots shown on television and the police violence was roundly condemned. The unrest went on well into the summer but, at our first assembly after that May bank holiday, Elaine welcomed those bruised and battered staff home as heroines. The revolt ultimately petered out, but not before it had shown the French establishment to be out of touch with the feelings of much of the country.

Mrs Porter's political beliefs came very much to the fore with me personally when in 1970 my year was the first eighteen-year-olds to get the vote. With the excitement of impending adulthood, it had been decided that the school would host hustings for all parties; one of them being the National Front. Given the demographic of the school this was difficult. My view as the person in charge of organising the event was that we should confront the party head on and show them for the fascists they were. One-third of the girls were Jewish and the prospect of this visit led to lively discussions.

Mrs Porter was completely against having them set foot in the school. One rainy day, in a cold and empty classroom, she and I had what can only be described as a screaming match. I have always believed in free speech and stood my ground; she was equally sure that I had no idea what I was unleashing. She had the power of arguments honed over years, I had my naive desire to do the right thing. In the end we agreed to differ, but after taking some more straw polls I decided that it would tear the school apart if the visit went ahead, so cancelled all meetings. Mrs Porter and I came away from our argument with an equal respect for one another which lasted throughout the rest of my time as her pupil.

'Are you the one who dissected the mouse on the kitchen table?'

It is almost fifty years later and I am at Elaine's funeral in Hastings.

I never joined the old girls' association but strangely was drawn into it by 'The Gentle Author', whom I had got to know in 2012, writer of the blog *Spitalfields Life*. He'd double-booked himself and was unable to attend the reunion that was taking place in what remains of CFGS in Spital Square, and asked me to cover it. La Chapelle is a magnificent Michelin-starred restaurant housed in the former chapel in which we'd had assemblies and where we attempted to perform gymnastics. After that event I kept in touch via social media, and in the summer of 2015 we heard of Elaine's passing.

The woman asking the question of me was Liz Cleere, the daughter of Dorothy Cleere who had taught me botany and zoology. The mouse in question had been brought in by one of the cats that inhabited the Cleeres' cottage near Wadhust in Sussex, to which I had been invited during the summer of 1968. Liz and her brother Chris were of primary-school age then and seemed completely unfazed by East End teenage girls being planted on them during their summer holidays. What possessed me to dissect the dead beast I cannot recall, but I do remember the event.

The cottage was everything one reads about of second homes owned by affluent people. Outside all wisteria and cottage garden, inside ramshackle, untidy and full of interesting books. We weren't there to pursue our studies, however, but to work. Henry, their father, was interested in archaeology. He worked in the iron and steel industry but this hobby, which would soon become his new profession, was the reason we were there. He sat and told us that he'd hired a helicopter to take aerial photos of parts of Sussex and, lo and behold, he thought there may be a Roman era iron smelting site at the bottom of the hill behind the cottage. I can still recall being shocked that anyone had the money to hire a helicopter, even more to waste it on such an endeavour, as I saw it.

That first night we sat in the honeyed aromatic darkness of a starlit evening in their garden overlooking the Weald. It was another world. Conversation flowed easily along with the food, home-made lemonade and wine. I couldn't help noticing that the house would have failed Mother's hygiene standards. Beneath the beds were tumbleweed-like balls of fluff and the surfaces were covered in a layer of dust. It didn't bother the Cleeres, whose house overlooking Clapham Common in London was pristine, undoubtedly courtesy of a cleaner. This was their place for relaxation and discovery.

The next day dawned bright and clear, as they did for the following two weeks. A digger had removed the topsoil and, armed with trowels and detailed instructions, we set to work. Soon it became apparent that Henry had been right: one of the other students also working with us uncovered the remains of a smelting oven and I found the slag heap of spent charcoal and oxidised fragments of materials that accompanied it. I spent hours in the heat sieving and sifting what to me appeared to be lumps of not very interesting stuff. Henry, though, was ecstatic and would pore over these items as if they were jewels. I would have been happy to have found a jewel or some pottery, but he appeared entranced by my slag heap discoveries. Nightly he sat in the garden with a magnifying glass, explaining the finds to us. The cottage became filled with box after box of finds. All meticulously labelled, they sat on shelves in a scullery area, then beneath beds and finally on any flat surface he could find.

Amid this Dorothy cooked and maintained the household in a warm and open manner. She was a good-looking woman with a lovely figure and an easy laugh, and I delighted in her company. Henry too was an attractive man, generous in praise and unlike anyone I'd met before. Towards the end of the second blistering week of working in the open air there was a cry from above. A neighbour, who had a far larger property than the Cleeres, had a swimming pool and he'd decided to empty it for cleaning. The void was above the dig, something he had only just realised as the water began to seep away. Henry, as if jet propelled, ran up the hill to try and do something. It was too late, the dig was flooded and soon we were standing in inches of muddy water.

Later that afternoon, wearing a swimming costume I had borrowed from Dorothy, Henry walked me along the wooded pathway which ran along the back of the cottage to the swimming pool, which we were now allowed to use whenever we wished. The costume was far too big and my small breasts wandered around inside the bra section uncomfortably. I felt equally uncomfortable by his proximity. I wasn't used to feeling much desire for anyone, or anything except my studies come to that. He may have noticed my awkwardness and possibly my desire, but if he did he certainly was too much of a gentleman to have acknowledged either. I do remember that he asked if I'd thought of doing archaeology at college as he felt I had a talent for it. I hadn't.

We chatted on about the future and the way I saw it going for me. I wanted to say that what I wanted was his life, their life, full of interesting people and interesting ideas. It took me a while to realise that this was what was attractive to me. He embodied a world of progress and possibility and, dare I say it, ease. Whether he was a self-made man or not I had no idea, but to him everything seemed possible.

As much as the school had played a huge part in my life I had no great feelings of regret as I left. I knew that it was time to move on. I was having a strip wash in the scullery at home when the letter arrived. It was before Mum went to work and she surprised me by being nervous as she handed it to me.

I ripped it open with a strange sense of dread and read that I had passed all three subjects well enough to go to university.

What to do?

Having had no parental or professional guidance as to a career path I thought that I would get a degree and hope that fate would intervene and sort out the future for me. The few fumbles I'd had with boys had already indicated that I might not be mating material and my antipathy to marriage was already in place.

The fact that I still spent much of my social life with my parents had been a cause for conversation in the common room as I had been asked about it by several mistresses. I had been persuaded by one of the mistresses that, rather than accept the place at the University of London to study geography and geology, instead I should go to Reading and study agricultural economics. The logic was that, as we were about to enter what would become the EU, the course would allow me to develop a career in Europe. The mistress saw my dependence on my parents as unhealthy, although she never put it quite so baldly, and leaving London as key to my development. I knew in my heart that she was right and so I agreed. For somebody who still thought that milk came out of bottles it was a bizarre choice to say the least.

Chapter 8

False Starts

Tony had driven Mum, Dad and me to the hall of residence that I was to live in for the first year of my university life. In 1970, there were so few cars on the road it took
less than an hour to drive from Bethnal Green to Reading.
The building was a crumbling Edwardian pile just off the
main road from the railway station. White Knights, the
campus itself, was a good twenty-minute uphill walk away.
The room I was given was on the top floor, four flights up
and next to the fire escape. It had two single beds, a gas fire
and a gas burner on which you could cook. It was bare and
depressing. When the family left I stared at it with a sinking
heart. On the first night there was a reception for the start
of the new academic year at which I figured out that I would
be using the gas burner quite a lot; the food served up made
school dinners seem like a gourmet experience.

I roomed with a girl from Leeds who was so sexually
mature that I found her, and her boyfriends, terrifying, but
I tried to settle into the rhythm of the place. I was bright
all right, but outclassed by a group of students to whom
privilege had seemingly come at birth and university simply
an opportunity to have a good time. Whereas I wanted to

work, they spent their days imbibing, sniffing and inhaling dubious substances, which often saw them end up in A&E. A hugely talented but disturbed girl called Dinah, who was studying my subject, killed herself with an accidental overdose. It was all so tragic and unnecessary. To my mind, university was supposed to provide me with a platform for living, not give me carte blanche for self-destruction. I'd received a small grant and would have to find work to supplement that; this degree was a serious concern to me, not a cause for frivolity. I sound like an arrogant stick in the mud, but that's how I felt.

As the term progressed I found my isolation almost intolerable, I simply did not connect on any level with anyone. I had to do something, so I joined the university choir. I had confidence in my voice, I'd been school soloist for a few years and had led the school in all of the major anniversaries which peppered one's year at CFGS.

Rehearsals were held in a large room in an old part of the university complex. It was hot and filled with stale air, painted a green colour which was almost grey it had been so long on the walls. I auditioned before the others arrived and the music master hadn't commented other than to accept me into the choir.

We were to perform at Christmas and there were several solo pieces to be sung in the concert. I'd noticed a buxom, ebullient woman with long dark hair when she'd entered the room as she was greeted by everyone; the star performer had arrived, and I'd had that moment of tingling in my arms when I knew something bad was about to happen. She bounced to the front and embraced the choir master then took her place. After some warm-ups and sing-throughs it was I, not she, who was given the definitive song to sing, 'The Last Rose of Summer', as a solo at the forthcoming concert. Her name was Isobel and she was apoplectic with suppressed rage at being usurped. She stared at me with uninhibited contempt and at the end of the rehearsal flew from the room with her coterie, leaving me behind with the non-sycophants.

'Isn't she just the one for histrionics.'

I raised my eyebrows.

'About time she was shifted down a peg or two.' He had a soft Irish accent and was called David.

We went for a drink together. He had black curly hair and a beard shot through with grey. A mature student and a former Catholic priest, he was kind and he made me laugh. We became friends, he roomed with another ex-priest, Patrick, and we three became a fixture. Going for walks and attending talks with them served to take the edge off the loneliness. David hinted at wanting more from our relationship, but only once did he make a move on me, and stopped himself when he realised that I was simply not interested.

Despite having someone to talk to as the term went on I found myself, more and more, getting the Friday night train back to Bethnal Green. I missed the warmth and the closeness of life with my parents. I missed understanding the geography, the jigsaw pieces that made sense of everything. They never questioned, never commented. They must have wondered, but my education had always been my choice so they left well alone. In the end I had a breakdown.

One Sunday afternoon in early December 1970 I sat crying and shaking in the kitchen at home. There had been no one inciting incident, but over the few short months the boil of my unhappiness had grown. My work went well, I didn't. Mum and Dad were nonplussed. Where was the girl who had stormed the heights of the grammar school system? The girl who knew exactly what she wanted and went out and got it? She had become this wreck, whose periods had stopped.

Being pregnant would have heaped such shame on my mother. Her mantra that she would put me out on the street still held. Much later I learned that both Nan and my grand-father were bigamously married so, in effect, Mum was illegitimate. It was a scar that destroyed much of her life, and all of her final years, such was the impact. On this occasion, she was comforted by the fact that the visit to Dr Marks to which she had frogmarched me resulted in my quivering confession of virginity. I was given a large horse pill of hormones to make me menstruate. I was no longer that four-year-old child and he was now a paler, greying version of the young man who had so loved my grand-mother, but he had stood the test of time in the East End and was as kindly as ever.

The next day I got on the train to Reading and cleared out my room. I never told anyone but left a note for my roommate. Nobody from home offered to come with me to help carry the bursting suitcase; education and the conse-quences it brought with it was still my own domain.

I recall the overwhelming sense of relief as I got on that train to Paddington. I bought myself a gin and tonic from the buffet car and breathed easily for the first time in months. I hadn't quite made it to the end of the first term and had no idea what I was going to do, but that didn't matter. I was going home.

I wasn't quite free of Reading University. Shortly afterwards a letter arrived. They had a counselling service, why had I not gone and spoken to them? I don't think I replied.

David, sweet soul, wrote me heartfelt letters and wanted to see me. I agreed and we met in central London for coffee. He was devastated that I hadn't revealed the depths of my distress. His former profession still directed much of his life and he was convinced that he could have helped me and wanted me to reconsider my decision to leave.

As much as I had wanted to work and succeed, the choice of my degree subject had been arbitrary and I was sure that something better would come along. By now David was part of the emotional landscape of a place I had no wish to revisit. I waved him onto the train back to Reading with no regrets at my decision.

Nervous breakdowns, sadly, don't disappear overnight and I spent the next three weeks sleeping most of the day. The stuffing had been completely knocked out of me, but in the East End you never admitted to feeling less than 100 per cent. The most that was said was that you mustn't grumble, this statement solely the province of the elderly who had multiple health problems. What people thought when I reappeared on the street I never knew. There had been no fanfare when I left, and as I had been around so much at weekends the odds were that nobody had really noticed my absence.

I was depressed but cocooned, and I have no idea how long that may have gone on, but one morning at eight I was delivered an ultimatum and a copy of the previous day's evening paper. Get a job and pay my way, or get out. Mother was always clear in her demands. No shirkers were going to live under her roof. With her threat ringing in my ears I sat staring at the situations vacant section. I needed to earn money and contribute to the home. I wasn't thinking of a career at that point, just survival.

I wanted something that would pay a decent wage. Of course, I could easily have followed Mum into the rag trade, but I had no desire to sit in cold, damp rooms and work machines that could maim you for life. Once when I had been working in one of the factories over school holidays an overlocker had got her finger trapped beneath the foot of the machine. I can still recall her screams of agony as attempts were made to free her. In the end she went off in the ambulance with her macerated finger still attached to part of the machinery. She lost her finger and much of her ability to earn a wage. They were hard lives and something reflective of a bygone era, or so I hoped.

Working as an assistant accountant may not have been earth shattering and I would have gladly wiped it from my memory except that it helped me realise that office work and I were meant to be strangers. Debenham Tewson & Chinnocks, or DTC, dealt in property, and as DTZ still does to this day. The best thing about their office was that it was next to St Paul's Cathedral on Paternoster Square. The worst thing about it was the same. Bell-ringing practice was both deafening and exhilarating. No concept of health and safety existed and you were expected to ignore the explosive boom which shook the windows and floors. It was yet another world.

I worked for a boss who was strangely another Wilkinson, but not one that I knew. He was a pale man with light-coloured hair and a gentle demeanour, and he sat in a glass-sided office the size of a shoe box. The area in which I worked was just outside of this.

My colleagues were Steve and Janet; Steve was a boy from north London with no accounting qualifications but tremendous talent. He was slender, wore slightly scruffy sandy-coloured suits the same colour as his hair, and smoked a lot. Janet was from one of the suburbs, she was always moaning about the trains. She was skinny with cascading dyed dark hair and big teeth.

As my mother was a dressmaker and as I was, as a consequence of my illness, slimmer than I'd ever been, I had become an attractive woman and my clothes were much admired. I never got over the absurdity of the morning make-up session in which all of the female staff virtually asphyxiated themselves with hair spray. They stood in front of a long mirror in the ladies, backcombing their hair into monstrous piles and slapping on inch-thick foundation followed by a storm of powder and blusher.

It wasn't so different to the boy and man talk I had been subjected to at university by the female students, except these girls seemed to have more fun. There were no hints of Descartes or Sartre in their conversations, just tales of jolly nights out in boozers by the river and night clubs. I never joined in and they thought me an oddball for sure. Even more so I never did anything to my hair and I really never put make-up on. I wore a bit of lippy and not much else, just like Mum, who as a raving beauty had never needed any embellishment. Not that I was in her league, but my father would have gone mad if I had gone out with more than a hint of colour on my face.

The work was dull and repetitive and I wasn't any good at it. It brought in a salary, that was the best I could say about it. I enjoyed the people and my credentials with them rose exponentially when I was spied out with a man.

One March morning the phone on my desk rang. It was Dad, he wanted to meet me for lunch. I don't believe that there is one boundary between childhood and becoming an adult. It seems to me that there are many watershed moments on the other side of which things will never be the same. The lunch we shared when I was at DTC was one. His illness when I was sixteen had been another.

I'd come home from school to find him in tears sitting in his kitchen armchair. A telltale puddle of liquid sat on the floor.

'I can't get up,' he said. 'I've been here all day.'

Eventually he was diagnosed with a strange form of arthritis. It wasn't quite ankylosing spondylitis, which progressively fuses your vertebrae, as there were more inflammatory aspects to his disorder. Therapy in those days was based on treating the symptoms rather than trying to get to the root cause; even today treatment of these disorders is problematic in the extreme. He was given pills which helped his mobility and he was soon back at work. Sadly, he was prescribed them for far too long and he began bleeding from his gut.

He spent months washing out his underpants in secret, getting the blood out of them. For men of his era the embarrassment of such was huge. It never occurred to him that the medication was to blame. In the end he all but collapsed from anaemia and the cause was found. In today's world, where bodily functions are broadcast in the media, it is hard to envisage the high levels of personal boundaries that existed between spouses such a relatively short time ago.

Slowly he began to seize up. His joints swelled and his skin erupted into psoriatic lesions and he was inevitably invalided off work.

'Lunch?'

'Why not? You do get a lunch break?'

It was an unusual invitation and one which came out of the blue. There had been no preamble at home, no testing to see if I was free at lunchtimes. I don't even recall him knowing my work phone number, yet here he was. As much as we had been close when I was younger, as an adult I had never been completely alone with him. There had always been an audience of some kind or another.

I named a place I thought he would like and wondered at this new turn in our relationship. I feared he was going to tell me that he was dying as he had been so terribly unwell.

That was not the case but that fear pushed me into a state akin to tunnel vision, and my memory of that meeting is dreamlike, fluid, as if time were halted to encompass its import. The players moving in slow motion, the script being improvised, the outcomes unknown.

This memory begins with grey. Streets, buildings, people. St Paul's Cathedral, coarsened by centuries of pigeon droppings, grey against a heavy March sky. Paternoster Square is the white-grey of new concrete. The cold is from a wind tunnelling past the empty shops and restaurants and down the stairs onto Cheapside, where it flattens a bed of newly planted geraniums rendering them anaemic and muddied.

The only colour belongs to you, Dad, sitting outside the bar with your face lifted to the sun. A pink shirt, warm and welcoming, two buttons undone, a sprig of hair jutting out and above it a cautious smile, a new smile. Conspiracy? Your full lips are wrapped around a roll-up. It is flattened at one end, brown with nicotine as you rest it in the ashtray. I sip the too-sweet sherry you have already bought and grimace. It is as brown as the tip of the cigarette as we study one another across the grey curl of smoke. The wind freed from the concrete tunnel seems suddenly warmer, human. You sip your drink and wait. Who says what to whom in this symphony of a moment? Beside us the buses flow north and south as the clock on the cathedral rings a solid one o'clock. I chew a white and yellow sandwich, Cheddar I suppose. You smile and point at the drink I have disowned.

Alone, I watch the greyness descend upon us. We have beaten the City suits by moments. Yours, I know, will be the only slash of colour at the bar at which you will now be fighting for a bottle of something. The sandwich is gone, I pick another. White with a thin strip of pink, ham I suppose. Your battle at the bar won, you bring a bottle of Muscadet, it is safe and not too expensive. You sip, finding the tilt of the head which the glass demands difficult. As difficult as the trip to the bar and back out into the courtyard had been. As difficult as not mentioning it is. As difficult as the pain which makes you hobble is.

Your suit is grey. Not the flat twill grey of the others as they fill the courtyard, but mohair. Black with threads of silver it shines metallic and hard. We talked but I don't remember the words. It was about journeys, that first time together as adults. You had noticed my difference from others, my trying to fit in. The hours of solitude at home have given you time to reflect on this daughter who arrived late in your life.

Your wrist was thinner than it should have been as you reached for the curling frond of another sandwich and then nodded towards the grey building in which I worked.

I shrugged. 'Passing time,' I said, 'I'm just passing time.'

Earning a wage and not going mad, stopping myself from going mad again, learning the tricks of survival. You didn't want that for me, I felt it rather than heard the words.

'Be yourself, be different. Don't give in.'

You never said 'don't be like me', but it was implied.

'I never helped, did I? When you were ill I mean.'

The pink of your shirt is suddenly too bright for my eyes in this grey world. Too real, like you at this moment.

'No,' I say, in all honesty.

'I'm sorry.'

I smile. We both know that he didn't have the armoury to cope, he never had. The final memory of that afternoon is red. The red of the bus as your solid leather shoe hit the platform, an eternity of balance and pain until the other foot joined it. Black shoes on black rubber as the belch of diesel filled the air and you were gone.

Our meetings became weekly. It was weeks, not months this new closeness; I had little doubt that my life as an accountant was limited and who knew where I may go after that. The pinks, greens, yellows and blues of his shirts fill my memory signalling a relationship that was hidden. Always in Mother's shadow because you chose to be; illness and time made you want to find the person you once were. Fear of this dreadful illness made you desperate, and I was your only hope because I would listen and not judge. I was still young, achingly young, but you clung to me and you talked. Lunches in a variety of quiet and ancient bars and cafes were tenuous at first, as if you were excavating yourself, looking for clues.

'Having all that time sitting, thinking, has been a bit of a curse.'

I nodded and asked about the war, wondering if like my uncle George he was suffering under the weight of an awful secret. He wasn't, but he had regrets. From the age of fourteen he'd worked for the Gas Light and Coke Company which was on the Regent's Canal, a mere ten-minute walk from home. During the war his skills as a gas fitter and builder of domestic gas ovens had led to him being trained by the navy to fix damaged aircraft. Apparently he'd passed a six months' course in six weeks and before he knew it was put on the *Queen Mary* liner and taken across the Atlantic. He had never been further than Ramsgate or Southend, so the sight of the Statue of Liberty was burnt into his memory. New York had enthralled him and coming from the land of nothing to the land of plenty was a shock. He didn't know where he was going after landing, or why. He liked New York, but soon found himself on a series of Greyhound buses heading south.

As he told me, civilisation soon disappeared and although Bethnal Green was far from multicultural, the mix of religions and the presence of the likes of Diamond Lil on the street made one understand difference. Segregated eating establishments and toilets he managed to tolerate, but when a pregnant black woman was denied a seat and asked to stand on the bus as all the 'colored ones' were full, Dad stood and surrendered his. Being in jail in Virginia overnight for disturbing the peace did not quell his hatred of the system. He made his destination in one piece and without a criminal record. It was Trinidad from where, he was told, they were to prepare for the invasion of Japan.

I have photographs of his time in the Caribbean, unusually for him, not many but enough. I never knew him to take a photo willingly, and apart from when Mother took her standard shots of floors or ceilings, the only photos we have are from when other family members wielded a camera. There is only one shot of him as part of a group of sixteen men outside of what I assume is their barracks, which is on stilts. He told me tales of using old tobacco tins filled with insecticide placed under the legs of their bunks to stop spiders getting into the bedding. He talked of a drunken fight that broke out in a bar between rival groups of sailors.

'I stood there and watched the silly sods beating the hell out of one another. They had their beers and rums lined up on the bar. I drank as many as I could and got out before the MPs arrived.'

He never talked of women, or of friends. He did talk of the exhilaration of repairing an aeroplane and going up in it, apparently this was to ensure they did their jobs properly. He loved the heat, loved swimming in the ocean, but never went back, or even expressed a desire to do so. Only once did I ever see him enter the sea. It was on the island of Jersey during a heat wave; he only went in knee deep, proclaiming it not warm enough.

His regrets centred on his lack of courage. He was a highly intelligent man and at war's end was offered a position as an engineer for the aircraft company De Havilland. He turned it down. Mother apparently was furious. They could have escaped the slums, escaped a family situation which meant that she was a skivvy to all and sundry, lived in the countryside in a house with hot water and a bathroom, but he would not be moved.

'Were you scared?' I asked him as we sat in an alcove of Short's Long Bar at the Aldwych, nursing schooners of sweet, nutty Amontillado.

He sucked on his cigarette.

'I don't know. I just couldn't do it. Your mum never forgave me, and maybe she was right. I should have had the courage.'

He had his routine, he had his family and he had his job back. He'd been lucky too, the Japanese were defeated by a bomb and Dad never saw action. For him that was enough.

During all of those conversations we never once mentioned Clara. She had died in 1968, leaving a small amount of money with which the family had gone to a holiday camp at Bognor Regis for Christmas. I have a firm memory of pushing my young nephew in his pram along the seafront and being enveloped in waves whipped up by the December storms. Our nights were spent in laughter and singing. It had felt strange having a good time when she had died so horribly alone. I could have brought the subject up, but what would it have served? Dad could not help me with how I felt about her now, just as he never could when she was living.

No, these lunches were about us and about him giving me some courage to rediscover myself; to be more like the teenager to whom anything had seemed possible. From time to time I glimpsed the carefree young man who had wandered around the West End with his friends, or sat in the pubs of the East End discussing politics. The 1930s had been a heady time, with Oswald Mosley and his Blackshirts attempting to bring the fascist message to the streets of England. Smoky coffee shops and communist groups peddling their propaganda on street corners vied with the splendour of hotels like The Ritz and Claridge's in his memory.

'We'd get dressed up to the nines and wander in, just to have a look about.'

He'd had a friend who was 'kind' to older rich widows and Dad would sit in the bar nursing a drink while the kindness was dispensed in a bedroom somewhere.

I wasn't shocked; surprised maybe that he was so open about it.

My life in accountancy came to an end when I somehow lost £10,000 from an account. My mind had wandered and some noughts had gone missing. It was a prestigious account too, an international company of some importance to DTC.

It took a fair while to discover from where I had made this loss and the mere effort of this bored me to distraction. Our calculators had rolls of tape and I searched back through I don't know how many before the slip was detected. I failed to see what all the fuss had been about, and Mr Wilkinson not so delicately suggested that I might be more suited to another profession.

Chapter 9

A Career in Science

My eyes were swimming, almost as much as the sperm in the sample that I was trying to count. I'd been working at the Royal Free Hospital haematology department for a few months before I was asked to take on the samples from the male fertility clinic. As a nascent science, there was no dedicated space for this apart from a consulting room somewhere nearby our laboratory and our toilet, which was now stacked with dubious magazines and sterile cups. Red-faced men emerged from here holding one of these fast in their hands before scuttling away down the stairs trying to remain as incognito as possible. We had no spare incubators in which to maintain these precious fluids at body temperature, so we'd keep them in our lab coat pockets or held between our thighs until they were processed.

My voyage to work in science was partly Mother's doing. Once again I had been mining the vacancy pages of the papers when she showed me a job that she had circled. 'You'd like that.'

The ad was for a trainee medical laboratory technician. Having studied in the antediluvian laboratories at school, the Nissen hut perched above the middle of the hospital forecourt presented few difficulties for me. It was arrived at by exterior metal steps, had little heating and was prone to rock in a high wind.

I began working there on a rather cold late spring day in 1971, and the first person I remember seeing was a scientist called Elsie Bahadursingh, who wore a red sari and a thick jumper beneath her lab coat, and fingerless woollen gloves. She sat at a microscope singing a high-pitched song in an Indian language. Her smile was as infectious as the laboratory was cold. 'Welcome,' she said, expiring a breath which was clearly visible.

It was a small space furnished with wooden furniture and wooden work benches, which had the blood stains of ages impregnated upon them. The bleach with which we liberally doused the surfaces may have sterilised them, but the rust-coloured patches were a permanent feature. Elsie gave me a whistle-stop tour of what seemed a very basic set-up and was just finishing when the head pathologist walked in. He was Professor Fleming and the myth was that he was Sir Alexander Fleming's son; a myth I imagined he'd concocted himself. He sported half-rim glasses over which he peered down at you; his smile was broad and full of badly aligned, brown and chipped teeth.

'Hello girlie.'

He came to stand at what I learned was a staining machine. Blood smears were put into holders which were circulated through baths full of solutions which stained the cells differing colours. It wasn't the machine that interested me, however. Prof. Fleming was using the flat surface of the machine as a desk on which to sign the haematology reports. This was all well and good, but on the underside it was also the carrier for the holders and as such rose and turned at predetermined, but irregular, intervals, and his precision in knowing exactly when to stand up and lift the documents was almost balletic.

The chief technician, Alan, was on first meeting full of a giggly laughter, which hid a shy nature. He sported a lush ginger moustache and sideburns to counter the growing baldness of his pate. At moments of agitation, or embarrassment, he blushed deeply while kneading his facial hair. His sidekick at work was the senior tech, Pat, who came from the north of England and was spectacularly irreverent. It was the kind of double act I saw many a time in science; Alan and Pat loved one another. He was married, she not, but he was a gentleman much, I imagine, to her annoyance. They were of a similar age, being in their late thirties, and frequently went for a drink together after work before going home. The Calthorpe Arms sat behind the hospital on a quiet side street and was Royal Free Central for socialising. Here Alan and Pat would sit chewing over the day's events, discussing the challenges that were key to keeping the laboratory running.

Even to my untrained eye, it was an underfunded establishment, and like many of the London teaching hospitals had satellite establishments whose upkeep ate into the central budget. Taking on work from another department brought in extra funds, which was why the fertility clinic had come within our purlieu.

Elsie sat next to me to check the sperm counts that I

attempted to perform. On these days, the laboratory took on the pungent odour of semen as we looked down the microscopes to try and count the 'swimmers'. If it was a lively sample that was difficult; the slower samples and the ones with two heads were easier to count. Sometimes as sperm ambled past you could almost name them, having seen them before on their slow trajectory in the opposite direction. The saddest were the 'dead' samples, in which there were plenty of sperm but they were immobile, or those with little or no sperm at all. I often imagined the difficult and painful conversations that took place as a consequence of my writing the statement: 'No motility observed.'

It was a hit and miss affair, but then much of laboratory science in the 1970s was based more on the experience of the staff performing the tests than any results a machine could generate.

A few years later, when at the London Hospital in Whitechapel, I worked on call with a man called Eddie Telfer. He was well past retirement age, but had lost his wife, so had come back to work nights to occupy himself. He was born in the early years of the twentieth century so had seen routine pathology almost from its inception. He'd served in the medical core during the Second World War and ended up in North Africa. Eddie would smell a sample of urine or sputum and sometimes faeces and be able to tell you exactly what the patient was suffering from.

'Remember, we had little or no equipment in the desert, smell was all,' he'd say, peering through his spectacles as he removed the lid of the pertinent receptacle. He'd then hold it a couple of inches below his nose to savour it with the satisfied expression that greets a good bottle of wine. We'd go through the motions of scientific testing but he was almost always right on first sniff.

Through him I learned about the North African desert and men who suffered a dizzying array of gastric and ear infections, which were often untreatable.

'At the start of the campaign we were losing four men from illness to each man from battle wounds,' he told me. With almost no treatment for diarrhoea it was an acute problem but one that was more easily solved than treating otitis media.

'Hygiene became our mantra, that and stopping the men eating in local places when on leave. The local water was a zoo.'

He never mentioned that sexually transmitted diseases topped the list of debilitating infections caught in the theatre of war, but then the diagnosis of that was purely clinical, based on the examination of the afflicted part of the soldier's anatomy and a question as to which bordello he had visited.

By this time I was rooted firmly in the scientific community that was medical laboratory sciences. From my earliest days at the Royal Free I knew that I had found my home. It was so different from my university days or my brief sojourn in accountancy. In the laboratory I felt that I was working with people with whom I had a common cause. The science was important, get it wrong and there were consequences far more important than losing a few noughts on the tally of an account. Each hospital had its own version of this family, and each of the London teaching hospitals had their own fields of expertise, and we had to understand the techniques needed to support them.

The Royal Free specialised in liver disorders, and for some time the Hepatic Group had been pioneering perfusion. Essentially, human blood from a patient in liver failure was processed through a pig's liver to cleanse it. At that time the procedure offered some hope to acutely ill patients; however, it was a short-lived technique which was superseded by the development of transplants. Nevertheless, it generated a lot of interest in the 1970s and one summer's day, during my first summer at the Free, a news film crew arrived to record the process. The demonstration, using a couple of units of human blood, a pump and a pig's liver which had been attached to a board and sat on an easel, was set. It had been decided to do this in a small courtyard in the grounds of the hospital; the surgeons had not been keen on filming a 'live' human perfusion.

I stood next to Alan, who as usual was gently massaging his moustache. The cameras rolled, the pumps began and we stood and waited. Alan's massaging became faster and he nudged me.

'Nothing's coming out,' he said. 'There must be a clot in it.'

At that moment the liver, now thrice the size it had been at the start, exploded over the assembled audience. A profound hush descended, the only sound coming from the blood that dripped from an engorged camera that had been in the line of fire. The lab staff took a collective in breath and unsuccessfully suppressed a howl of laughter. Needless to say, we never made the six o'clock news.

*

The hepatitis B virus had been discovered in 1965 and HIV was well in the future. Yet even though the Royal Free was at the forefront of treating hepatic disorders, we happily ate our lunch and drank tea at the bench and smoking was common. If you did scratch yourself with a glass pipette or needle that had been in contact with a hep patient, you were subjected to a large bolus injection of immunoglobulin in a solid adjuvant into your backside. I've had two of those and it's something you don't forget, as walking is difficult for days afterwards and sitting a nigh-on impossibility.

Apart from Alan, Pat, Elsie, Prof. Fleming and myself there was a technician called Olympia, Olly for short, a swarthy Greek girl with an amazingly low but mellifluous voice; Gordon, a young man whose mother worked as a medical secretary for the hospital; and various doctors on circulation through the pathology labs. The sample receptionist was a woman called Gwen who weighed in at some twenty-plus stone; she was supported by an older Austrian lady called Elsa who had escaped the Nazis. Elsa still had an accent as rich as treacle and a tremor to her hands that had nothing to do with her age. Gwen's husband Bill ferried the samples from source to laboratory and delivered any pathology-related materials wherever they were needed. His vehicle was a beaten-up Ford sedan which he kept going with a wing and a prayer. He complemented his wife almost exactly in the weight stakes. Gwen's tiny room was directly opposite the toilet and although music was not allowed to be played at work, she was permitted to listen to Radio 4 on fertility clinic days to drown out any untoward sounds that might emanate from the attempts to produce a sample.

For once my A levels were of use. I was able to bow out of the first part of the course to qualify as a medical laboratory scientist and go straight to the Higher National Certificate. The classes were held at Paddington Technical College and the evening practical aspect at the London Hospital's medical school laboratories.

The arc from wood to Corian bench surfaces, from using your finger to slow down a centrifuge to waiting for a series of locks to permit entry to your sample, encompasses my time in laboratories. Some would see this as going from amateur hour to cutting-edge high tech, but I see it differently. It seems to me that we now drown in regulation and forget the basics of the craft that science really is.

The London Hospital evening classes were run by a maverick group of old-school types, all male, who never wore lab coats, turned up drunk and smoked throughout the lectures they gave. Like Eddie Telfer, they'd all done their time in the services during the Second World War and had more tales to tell than scientific expertise, or so it seemed to me at the time. Years later I appreciated their propensity to go off-message greatly, as their abilities to join up apparently invisible dots in techniques gave me the insight to develop some novel techniques in my own field of work.

There was one man whose name I simply cannot recall, although I can see him clearly. Over six feet tall he was a commanding presence. He wore a dark blue suit and a waistcoat with a gold fob-watch on a chain strung across it. He smoked constantly and lectured us on the structure of haemoglobin and the disorders that arose when it was defective. He carried an old, rusted nail in his pocket. I always imagined it had been used at a crucifixion, so hooked and twisted it was. 'This is the amount of iron present in the human body,' he would say with relish placing it on a bench. 'Not much, is it?'

If the haematology lab was small at the Free, the blood transfusion lab was a broom cupboard which was overseen by Patricia, as opposed to Pat. It was a thin tongue of a room, with the blood fridges on the right, a space for two technicians to sit on the left and Patricia's space at the end facing the window. It was tucked above a stairwell and beside a small lecture theatre in which luminaries like Professor Norman, the head of the liver unit, gave talks. She was yet another Patricia and was a force of nature in the medical world of the day: forthright, opinionated and fiercely protective of her patients, most of whom sadly did not survive coming to her as they did so with end-stage diseases. I remember her crying at the death of a lovely young woman who had wanted to be a model. She had split up with her boyfriend, taken an overdose of paracetamol, a very large overdose. On recovering briefly from her coma she had declared that all was well and that she wanted to live, but her liver was so damaged that she died.

I can still hear Prof. Norman saying over and over again, 'What a waste.'

'You can always repeat a blood count but you cannot retrieve a unit of blood once it has been transfused,' was the first and essentially the most important mantra with which I was welcomed to Patricia's realm.

She was a nervous woman in her forties and had long brown hair, flecked with grey. She wore spectacles, had a slight lisp and a slighter limp with her right leg. Her empire was so small that she could swivel her chair around and pick up almost all that she required without standing.

I'd been doing blood groups for about a month when I was allowed to perform my first crossmatch. I had heard tales aplenty by this point of mishaps due to mislabelling or lack of attention to detail, which had resulted in a patient receiving a unit of blood that did them more harm than good. Deaths were not unheard of. I shook as I performed the task, with Patricia looking over my shoulder. The procedure entailed incubating patient serum with cells from the units of blood they were to receive. This was performed in a range of laboratory environments. A crossmatch also entailed looking for antibodies present in that patient serum against a panel of indicator cells, to see if anything obscure might be present. This was all done at differing temperatures and with the aid of enzymes and other reagents to coat or strip the erythrocytes (red blood cells) to make the test as sensitive as possible.

The woman I had crossmatched for was to have an elective hysterectomy the following day. She might or might not need a transfusion. That night I didn't sleep. I went over and over the procedure I had performed in my mind, looking for potential pitfalls or things I might have omitted to do.

Patricia was always in early, and the following day was no exception. I began to work, but couldn't restrain the temptation to open the blood fridge. The two glass bottles with my handwritten labels on them had gone. My stomach hit my throat.

'She was first on the elective list at eight, and yes, she bled,' Patricia said, and swivelled around to look at me. 'I'll check how she is later and then you can go and see her.'

'Why?'

'You know why. To prove you didn't kill her.'

She smiled at me broadly. I nodded. A rite of passage had just been passed.

The woman was tall, almost as tall as Alan, and stooped somewhat. She wore a stylish white raincoat and she was heading our way. I went back into the lab and reported to Patricia. We were one short in blood transfusion. The bench which I had appropriated for one was meant for two, and that other person was to be a senior technician. Alan brought her in for Patricia to interview.

I could tell that the shoebox of our abode was not what she had expected. After almost a year of occupation I hardly noticed its shortcomings. The trailing electric wires to the ancillary fridge in the corridor, the peeling paint on the ceiling, the absolute lack of space. We did good science in there, or so I believed, and that was all that mattered to me. I noted the black hair, the intense deeply set brown eyes and an unseasonal suntan, before Patricia raised an eyebrow and I left to huddle with Gwen over a cup of tea.

'Well?' I asked half an hour later.

Patricia sniffed, her nervous version of Alan's moustache kneading. 'She's very well qualified.'

My heart sank, I loved our world. True some days we were run off our feet, but with the occasional help from Olly we managed.

'The Prof. thinks we should up our game.'

I snorted and looked at Patricia.

'I know,' she said. 'Who needs his opinion.'

Prof. Fleming was a showman of whom I had learned to be wary. Always one for a story or a bon mot, one day when I helped him draw a pint of blood from a donor to cover an operation he had lost the plot, or rather the plot had overtaken him. The good doctor was in such full flow of his tale that he forgot to clamp the tubing in the man's arm when he severed it. The remaining tube which was under pressure from a cuff spun blood in perfect circles over the walls and ceilings of what was our coffee room. Luckily the man had his eyes shut and I rushed to clamp the remaining tube and release the pressure. Prof. Fleming, with his back to us, was still recounting his tale. On turning and observing the newly decorated surfaces he'd had the good grace to pale and then blush, and I spirited the donor into the corridor before the events became apparent. I returned to clean up as best I could, just as he was finishing labelling the unit.

He looked at me with curiosity.

'Calm under fire, aren't you girlie?'

I was washing the walls by this point.

'Shall we keep this to ourselves?'

I nodded.

He patted me on the backside and left.

'How up our game?'

'Oh, she's been working in some fancy lab in Italy, or somewhere. Trained at the North Middlesex.'

'Well, that will hardly set the world on fire.'

We looked at each other. I don't set much stock on astrology, but we were both Pisceans and shared certain traits, most particularly that our little world was precious to us. It was a place we could both survive within. Patricia rented a small flat in Islington and I was still at home. She and I didn't socialise with one another, but our days were spent in friendly conversation. I knew that she lived with a much younger man called Jeremy, who played the guitar and paid no rent. My upbringing made me wary of those who did not pay their way, but Pat loved him and it was none of my business. Apart from Jeremy, work was her world and she was fearful of change within it.

Jenny, the new senior technician, was to begin work the following week. I cleaned and scrubbed. Patricia straightened up the notices that were stuck to the walls. We even had a go at sorting the trailing wires to make them less obviously lethal. At the bottom line, Patricia, of course, was afraid of losing her job. She was a good, basic technician with years of experience. She wasn't, however, curious to learn more and there was a lot more to learn. The demographics of London were changing hugely, bringing with it challenges to the diagnostic aspect of our profession. Prof. Fleming, for all his bombast, was actually right to bring in new blood.

Hindsight is 20/20 for sure, but nobody ever has the chance to use it. I'm not saying I should never have become involved with Jenny. No, we had far too much between us to say that, but persistence being one of my personality traits doesn't always serve me in good stead.

At first Jenny wasn't much for conversation, or gossip, a bit of a closed book really. She didn't come over as shy, just a bit officious at first, but it didn't take me long to realise that she was lonely.

She was two years older than me, but rather than mess around as I had with university and dead-end jobs, she'd gone straight into laboratories from school, climbed the qualification route and then gone off to live and work in Italy.

I gleaned this over the first couple of months in which she worked with us. During that time Patricia's antipathy mellowed and she actively engaged with the changes that Jenny suggested. New reagents appeared and new equipment began to replace ancient examples that no longer worked efficiently. I knew that Patricia had been requesting these replacements for a good while; if their appearance rankled, she never said. Perhaps she played it cleverly, realising early on that Jenny wasn't one for longevity anywhere so she might as well get all she could from the situation.

Slowly, Jenny and I began a dance that ended in a complex relationship which lasted thirteen years. I can't honestly recall how things evolved or what attracted me to her in the first place. Initially it was our joint need for companionship.

I began to stay over at her parents' house in north London, which had a bathroom, and she would stay at ours, which of course still did not.

Her family life was riven with strife. Her father and mother had a fractured relationship, which centred on him being intelligent and a professional, and she who, unable to cope with her own shortcomings, had become a nervous wreck. She, Irene, had been a lovely looking woman from a working-class background similar to my parents. Her husband, Jock, was from Aberdeen and a pharmacist. They had met when he'd come down to London and they had married. It was a mismatch of the first order, and by the time I met them they were barely on speaking terms. There is no doubt at all that Irene was a depressive in an age before it was acknowledged. Jock was completely opposite. Outgoing and worldly wise, he was intellectually frustrated by the situation that he found himself in.

I suppose given all of this it was no surprise that Jenny's younger sister suffered from an acute form of anorexia with which she terrorised the household. Everything within her world was ordered, filed alphabetically and neat. If any one thing was out of place she raged and smashed things.

My upbringing may not have been as smooth as silk, but I had never been exposed to such a difficult situation. Even Clara's plight had not traumatised the whole family as much as this.

Not surprisingly, Jenny stayed more and more at my home. By then, with Tony long married, his was now a spare room which she claimed as her own. Jenny might have represented the sister I never had, but she didn't. I came to realise that I desired her physically. It wasn't a revelation to me, but it was something that I didn't know how to handle. To conform to the old cliché, I thought I was on my own in feeling this way. I knew that while in Italy she'd had relationships with men and she certainly never gave out any signals that she was interested in me sexually.

Nevertheless, our friendship deepened. She fell in love with my part of London, different as it was from the ordered streets and duplicate houses from whence she came. My parents accepted her presence without comment, other than she seemed like a 'nice' girl and they were glad I was making friends.

We talked endlessly into the night about the world, philosophy and our work. She was a companion in every way, someone to go to the theatre, exhibitions and on holiday with. Someone to learn from and to study with, someone who filled a void.

I'd been at the Royal Free for eighteen months when I decided to move on to pastures new. I had been studying at Paddington College and had met people who worked in other hospitals which had top of the range equipment and laboratories that were not the size of broom cupboards. As much as I loved working with Patricia, I needed to be stretched, and no matter what changes had been made I felt that the Free was not going to deliver for me. By now I had accepted that science was a career in which I belonged, and I wanted to make the best of it.

In late 1972 I went to work at the London Hospital, which was a twenty-minute walk from home. Compared to the Free the labs were vast and at the cutting edge of our profession, using techniques we could only have dreamt of in our Nissen hut. It was here that I met Eddie Telfer, but I spent much of my time in blood transfusion where I worked with one of the unsung heroines of science, Margaret Kenwright.

Margaret was a dragon to most people. She was from the north of England, Manchester to be precise. She was in her

fifties and overweight, with spindly legs that seemed to struggle to support her more-than-adequate frame as she tottered
the length of the corridor to where the freezers were housed.

Freezers are very important and their maintenance a job
not to be taken lightly. Margaret's cache of unusual, exotic
and irreplaceable samples were her children, and woe betide
anyone who did not check the temperatures daily and accurately.

Her hair was a wig, or rather several, which she rotated
when needed. The perennial cigarettes that she smoked and
the gin she so loved to imbibe resulted in the loss of her
hairpieces in taxis and various pubs, or up in flames.

She was also a diabetic and she kept insulin in one of the
blood bank fridges in her office-cum-laboratory. My first
introduction to her was when she was injecting herself with
her midday dose through her stockinged thigh. She wore
pebble-thick glasses through which a pair of tiny, bright blue
eyes twinkled.

In a world which even back then was dominated by male
medics, somehow Margaret glided above them all. She was a
scientific free spirit and saw no obstacles to her lowly qualifications supporting high aspirations – as far as I know she
had only basic qualifications and no degree either scientific or
medical. Her greatest gift was not seeing barriers. Connections
were there to be made and it mattered not a jot that you mixed
various disciplines to investigate or to prove a point.

So it was that I went from using the formalised techniques taught me at college and the Royal Free to a form
of well-controlled mayhem. Not that everything was not
recorded and scrupulously checked, it was the sheer extent

to her lateral thinking, no doubt based on experience, with which she continually surprised me.

The London was in the middle of a population that was Bengali, Jewish, Irish and smatterings of everything else. The ante-natal clinic had a large cohort of black women who presented us with some interesting challenges as they progressed through pregnancy. One of these was a tendency to produce cold agglutinins, which are antibodies that react at below body temperature. If a transfusion was required, the infused blood had to be maintained at 37°C or it would essentially form clumps within their bodies and possibly kill them. Routine infusions happened at room temperature at best, so special heating equipment was recommended. Budgets were tight and in the absence of a heater the top of a radiator had to suffice.

There were far more esoteric antibodies which we discovered during our work, which Margaret took great delight in having analysed. I wasn't high enough up in the echelons those days to mix with the doyens of the immunological world, but she often visited the Lister Institute and worked with Robin Race and Ruth Sanger. These two individuals spent their lives working on human blood groups and Margaret would take them samples which we had identified as far as we could to see if they could identify what we could not.

One notable day I was grouping blood for someone who needed a fairly urgent operation and discovered that I had a group O Bombay on my hands. This is extremely rare and is where the subject is absent in any A, B or O type, so having antibodies to all, and thus unable to be transfused with any blood other than from another with the same group.

I stared at the result and repeated the typing. I repeated it another time just to make sure, before presenting the results to Margaret.

She peered at me through a haze of cigarette smoke.

'Are you sure?'

I nodded.

'How sure?'

'Three times sure.'

'Go bleed the patient yourself and do it again.'

She sat and watched me. Then, and this was unheard of, she tested it herself.

'OK. Well done.'

We had to get blood flown in fresh from India, where the group is present in 1/10,000 of the population as opposed to 1/1,000,000 in Europe.

The identification of O Bombay had required the use of a variety of absorption techniques not routinely used in other laboratories. This ability led to us being used by the forensic department of the Met Police to identify blood groups from cadavers, particularly those involved in fatal fires. The smell of semen with which my career had started was replaced by the smell of smoke, but luckily the samples were seldom of human tissue, instead mostly of liquefied blood.

Margaret was married to a lecturer at one of the technical colleges which taught biomedical sciences. She was a little older than him, but not by much and, rather like her, he was no oil painting. He popped into the lab from time to time and I found him indescribably bland. Once while in her cups, Margaret described how he had seduced her when she was at a conference. Large amounts of alcohol were involved and her wig fell off during the onslaught.

This image would not leave my mind on the evening that I found her dissolved into tears in her office. A half-demolished chocolate éclair sat next to a glass of what I assumed was neat gin. Curls of smoke hung in the air and her ashtray overflowed onto her desk. I knew they had only been married a few years, she and Douglas. Rumours of him using her as a stepping stone were standard coffee room gossip. I did from time to time point out that it was she who was the more renowned of the two, only to be shouted down by the feral desire to see an unattractive woman ridiculed.

I was on call and needed to spin down a unit of blood to pack the cells. I stopped at the sight of her and stared; she waved me towards the centrifuge which sat in her room. While I programmed it I searched for words. I could not ignore her distress. I turned to look at her, but she beat me to it.

'Tell the coffee room gossips that they won their bets. Douglas has left me.'

She waved at a chair and I sat opposite her.

'It's not my business.'

'No, but you are one of the few to see it like that. Why's that I wonder?'

I thought about all the secrets I had been told in the past and the secret that I held within myself.

'I come from the East End,' I said, avoiding any attempt at any sort of sane explanation.

'They don't gossip there?'

I smiled and shrugged. 'I learned not to stick my nose in. Never gets you anywhere.'

She smiled and took a swig of her gin and a bite of the éclair.

'And you never warn me about my diabetes, do you?'

'Same difference.'

'Not curious at all?'

I remained silent as she told me he'd left her a note. He'd gone off with a very much younger scientist.

'She's got a professorship, so more money in the kitty. Dear old Dougie, so bloody predictable.'

Despite the humour, she was bereft and I was unsure that she should be left alone. 'Shall I come back and sit with you?'

'Thanks. Eddie's coming in.'

She and Eddie Telfer went back a long way.

'Good.'

The unit of blood had spun down and our conversation was coming to a close.

'You will tell the others?' she asked, as I unloaded the centrifuge.

'If you want me to.'

'I do.'

The next day I did as she asked and watched the unkind humour explode around the coffee room. It was driven by inadequate men who would never attain anything like the stature that Margaret had within the scientific community.

Late in the afternoon I told her that the deed was done. She thanked me by taking me to the pub and grilling me for about an hour on my understanding of the Lewis blood group system. It was her way of showing that she cared.

Chapter 10

The Grand Tour

Once I had gained the next qualification towards becoming a senior medical laboratory scientist, I decided to throw in my job and go travelling. On 13 July 1974, I set sail from Southampton on what I hoped would be a life changing Grand Tour. By November 1974 I was back in London and looking for work.

The idea had been for Jenny and me to travel through Europe and then get a boat from Greece, or somewhere in the Mediterranean, and go to South America and find work. I'd had all the jabs and was ready for an adventure, except I hadn't actually reckoned on my mimicking Mother in one unfortunate respect, seasickness. She could be sick on Victoria Park boating lake and it looked as if I was the same. I had never been on so much as a fishing boat and I had assumed that like my father I would have sea legs, but no. We'd taken a ferry from Southampton to Bilbao. It being July of course there was a force 9 gale and I spent virtually the whole trip being very unwell. Finally, I slid down the wall outside the main reception on the boat.

Someone in officialdom, I don't know who it was as I had my glasses in my pocket, gave me a large globular object.

I asked for water with which to take it to be told it was a suppository. Trying to insert it during the gale requires no description, other than to say there were several near misses. After half an hour I was able to go to my bunk and lie down and sleep. Goodness knows what was in it but it saved me from jumping overboard.

With this on my mind, I wasn't too bothered when Turkey invaded Northern Cyprus and for the next few weeks shipping all but came to a halt. By this point in time we had journeyed from northern Spain, through central and southern France, and into Italy, where we would spend the majority of our time.

We had saved up for the trip, but Jenny was a real stickler for economising, something I have never relished. Growing up without doesn't mean you want to keep scrimping. We'd eaten tomato sandwiches on various beaches, washing it down with tap water. She'd find the cheapest accommodation so that our trip would last as long as possible. It was summer, it was hot and it apparently didn't really matter that beds were uncomfortable, the rooms were noisy and the other clientele suspect.

In Pisa we found a room in a student hostel where she had stayed once before and where we in turn stayed for some time. I fell in love with Pisa and Florence and the nearby coastal resorts of Massa and Viareggio. Jenny introduced me to some of her old connections and boyfriends and I began to learn the language.

One surreal night we were invited to a football match. It was outside of Pisa in the hills and a few of her friends were playing. Afterwards we went into a scruffy building which I assumed was a community hall, where a group of ancient men sat playing instruments I had never seen before. Horns and hurdy-gurdies are the closest I could come to describing them. There was very little light, except from an open fire, and the home-made wine was strong. The younger men began to dance, it was a little like the way Greeks danced, yet not. The rhythm was different and the movements more sexualised, homoerotic. The shadows loomed large on the walls as the dancers encircled the room. I recall loaves stuffed with meat and fish being on offer, and more wine. We were the only two women there and we were superfluous in every way.

Once we had exhausted the north of Italy, we decided to head south. By this point in the trip I was tiring of trudging from basic lodging to basic lodging, but my travel partner seemed to thrive on it. Of course, we had different experiences of home life and she had nothing stable to return to. I missed home inordinately and any time I managed a telephone conversation with Mum I felt a real sadness. I could see her perched on the small stool that sat next to the phone they'd had installed on the stairwell. She would be bathed in the soft yellow glow from the gaslight which still lit that part of the house.

What Mum thought of this trip she never offered, but she tried to sound interested in something she surely would never have wanted to do. After years of hard graft and poor living conditions, holidays to her were a moment of luxury, not the impecunious wandering I seemed to have undertaken. By the end of August I wanted to go home, but there was one final throw of the dice in the trip; something which made it worthwhile and without which I would have consigned the whole experience to the lowest corridors of my memory.

We were back in Florence and looking at the situations vacant in the English section of a local newspaper. One advert seemed to offer a chance at making some relatively easy money, but you know what they say, if it looks too good to be true. The ad in the newspaper was looking for people to sell books door to door. They were good books; historical, illustrated tomes produced by a firm called Mondadori. It seemed all legitimate and above board. We phoned the number and booked our place on a course run by a Mr Warner, which was being run in a hotel in the nearby town of Pistoia.

Reg Warner was a short middle-aged chancer strangely also from Bethnal Green. He had peroxide-dyed hair and a boyfriend, Gordon, whose black hair looked similarly bottle enhanced, but who was many years younger. I don't know what Reg's real profession was. I can't believe it was anything legal, but other than catch him with a bit of weed I never saw anything untoward, except of course the fact of his homosexuality which was illegal in Italy at that point. He had no Italian, Gordon did that. There were twenty or so of us and I was the least experienced Italian speaker, although everyone had to speak English as Reg did the training.

It wasn't made explicit when we signed up, but until we were accepted on the course we had to pay our own expenses. Having just partaken of the most expensive meal of our trip and registered the cost of the comfortable hotel room, which had an en-suite bathroom, Jenny was not impressed.

I had tried to find out where Reg's family were in Bethnal Green. He'd offered the information about his roots before I had told him mine, and from that moment on he was a closed book.

But he was a good salesman and a good trainer. We were paired up and shown how to persuade customers to sign up to a mini equivalent of *Encyclopaedia Britannica*. In class I was seemingly good at it and somehow we were sanctioned to become part of his team.

I felt uncomfortable, for although friendly I was awkward in some situations and cold selling was one of them. We were dropped off in small towns and hamlets to try and sell the books. Sometimes we had a list of places to visit, often not. It took three days before I managed to sign someone up and it became obvious that I was going to have to work very hard to close deals. The group became smaller as others found selling equally difficult, and as a consequence Reg became more strident in his top-up training sessions.

One dismal rainy day Jenny and I entered a car mechanic's shop to have the owner's dog attack us. Luckily the dog was small, the owner of the firm handsome, and nobody was badly injured. He had a friend, a one-legged doctor, whom he called in as the pooch had bitten Jenny on the ankle. Her wound dressed, coffee in hand, we told them about Reg. Marco, the owner, was one of those well-connected types upon which small villages and towns thrive. He knew everyone and everything that was going on in the locale. 'Did we want to work?'

We did, and after he'd made a phone call we claimed our luggage and were soon being whisked up to the mountains in a top of the range automatic BMW, which the doctor drove at break-neck speed. I suppose it was risky; we really had no idea who these men were, or where we were going.

Campo Tizzoro sits in the hills above Pistoia, one of the villages on the road to the ski resort of Abetone. When we arrived it was late afternoon and dusk had fallen. The village stretched away up the hill. It appeared to be a ribbon development of squat houses and small shops all abutting directly onto the road. The air was crisp and clear and the mountains stood in stark relief against a twilight sky. It was beautiful.

We were taken to the Albergo Tripolitania. It hardly seemed a tourist resort, but the hotel was of a substantial size and supposedly there were two vacancies for live-in staff. It was an echoing barn of a place, with a marble staircase and floors. Some of the paintwork needed attention but it wasn't squalid, just a little tired around the edges.

Manolo, the owner, appeared. He was a short, swarthy man who chewed on a cigar. He gave us the Tuscan equivalent of the evil eye as he fired off a succession of questions. In the end he crossed his arms and called for his wife, Liliana. She emerged in a whiff of garlic, wiping her hands on a tea towel. She was friendlier, but still wary.

'What's going on?' I asked Jenny.

'They need two waitresses who will also clean the rooms.'

'Bed and board?'

'And some cash in hand?'

It was illegal, we should have had visas to work.

'Is there a problem?'

'I think the last two played around with the men in the village.'

Liliana looked us over and fired off some more questions when an ancient, tiny woman who sported an enormous cardigan ambled into the conversation. She stood observing for a while before coming over and asking my name. I responded in my best Italian. She had small, inquisitive, sparkling blue eyes and as she smiled a gold tooth glinted at me.

'You look hungry.'

I smiled a yes as she put her arm around me and marched me towards the kitchen.

Behind me Manolo called out, 'Mama, I haven't finished.'

'They are all right, Manolo,' she threw over her shoulder as she squeezed mine warmly.

There were many things that puzzled me about the situation that we found ourselves in, the biggest being what were we employed to do?

The next morning the old lady, Nonna, for all her age, was the person who showed us how to clean the occupied guest bedrooms, all three of them. She joyfully threw bucketsful of water up the walls of the showers and showed us how to make the beds properly. The rooms were sparse and impersonal, almost monastic, and all taken obviously by men. As we swept and polished, enticing smells began to waft upstairs from below.

By 11 a.m. we'd finished the cleaning and headed down to the kitchen, which was a frenzy of activity. Domenico was a chef who came in at lunchtimes. He smiled a greeting at us from his great height of five feet. He was stirring a pot of sauce. Liliana and Manolo were boiling tons of pasta and we were set to slicing tomatoes for a salad. It was a well-practised routine; even Nonna played her part, she sat shelling peas. Most of the activity was around an island oven and gas burners which sat in the middle of the room, overhung by a large extractor fan.

I sneaked a peek in the dining room, or rooms I should say. One was large and all windows and housed the bar, the second was small, with bench seats and long tables. Every place in both was laid with cutlery and glasses. Carafes of wine were placed at intervals.

I was staring out of a window when a hooter sounded. The deserted main street suddenly became London Bridge during the rush hour. It was filled with a phalanx of humanity coming our way, for lunch.

What nobody had mentioned during the few hours we had been there, was that the village had been built solely to support a munitions factory and the hotel to serve as restaurant and accommodation for visitors to it. All seventy people that were approaching were to be served a three-course meal, wine and coffee, corrected with the liqueur of their choice in forty-five minutes. This was no set-meal scenario as personal preferences were catered for.

The larger, airy dining room, the *salle*, was for the white-collar workers, a mixture of engineers, secretaries and administration staff; the smaller room was filled to bursting with the *operai*, the workers, who wore overalls, caps and had big ebullient voices.

At first we served in the *salle*, where the talk was muted and an air of gentility prevailed. There were a handful of women to serve, but in there it was mostly men who wore classy suits and sported even classier haircuts. There was the pasta of the day with a range of sauces, or none. If it were none we had to provide it glazed with just enough olive oil to make it acceptable. Only some people liked more oil than others. The second course was a nightmare for me. In a place and time where everyone ate meat, you'd have thought that one main would be the order of the day, but no. Every day there was a special, but if you didn't want that you could order a cut of pork, veal or beef. Chicken was still a relative luxury and venison appeared only occasionally. Some had thick cuts of meat, others thin. Some liked their veal with Marsala sauce, some didn't. Luckily sweet was fruit and a cut of cheese, but yes, you had to know which cheese individuals liked, similarly for the liqueur in the coffees.

I had a fair few mishaps. As people had nicknames for the cuts of meats they liked one day I gave the managing director pork, not beef. On another day, I was so nervous that I dropped some pear peelings as I was clearing the table. Not a great crime, perhaps, but in those days of big turn-ups on trousers some peel became lodged in one owned by yet another manager, and I had to crawl on the floor to retrieve it.

I don't know if there were complaints about me, but soon I was working with the *operai*, where I felt much more comfortable. It seemed that language didn't matter so much as warmth of attitude. It felt familiar and welcoming. I was teased, my bum pinched and generally treated as a welcome addition to the scene. Liliana flitted between the two rooms making sure that things ran smoothly. My mishaps diminished and I found myself enjoying the company of the men.

After the mayhem was over and they had gone back to work, we assembled around the table in the kitchen to eat. Domenico was delighted to have new people to cook for and I took great delight in eating whatever he put in front of me. His spaghetti carbonara has never been bettered and his roast beef with rosemary lives on in my memory.

Liliana was no slouch in that territory. She cooked the à la carte meals for casual diners during the week, and on Sundays she rose at 5 a.m. to make the pasta for her legendary lasagne.

This pinnacle of family life, Sunday lunch, was a relaxed affair. The *salle* would usually be half full and there was a menu from which diners did not deviate. We served the lunch during which we had time to chat with the clients, most of whom were men that we served during the week and their families. It was usually the *operai* who came in; I imagine the white-collar workers went to the coast for their weekend's entertainment.

Manolo continued to give us the evil eye. He was a silent, taciturn man who only seemed to relax after several grappas. One morning I came down to the kitchen early to find him sitting with a rifle. Packets of shot lay on the table, no doubt made in the factory up the road. He and I were alone and he noted my surprise with a smile.

'Never seen one of these?' He shook the gun at me.

I'd never been in such close proximity to a firearm and I found it unsettling. He sipped an expresso and after I had made one for myself he asked me to sit with him. He asked me what my home was like. He never usually spoke unless about work and had certainly never shown any interest in us other than as tools to keep his business going.

My Italian was much better by now, so I told him about

Columbia Road, about how the shops here reminded me of there, which they did. They were small and the people who ran them friendly. How the labyrinth of the community in the village was familiar and how much I felt at ease within it. I told him what Mum and Dad did and talked about London, which he had never seen. I think he was surprised by my humble background. They'd had sundry girls pass through their doors, many of them English who, like us, were taking a gap year of sorts. His view of the Brits was of the jolly hockey stick upper-class brigade and not somebody like me.

Inevitably as I spoke about the East End the war was mentioned. Beneath the factory in Campo Tizzoro lay a complex of air-raid tunnels which had protected the workers when the allies bombed. The factory had been an important producer of arms for Il Duce. I wanted to ask Manolo what he had done during the conflict but I didn't dare. I knew the area had been a focus of partisan activity and he would have been the right age to have resisted the Germans. I thought if he'd been a part of that he would have mentioned it, so assumed that he'd probably fought for Hitler.

'A terrible time,' was all he said about it, and he continued to polish his weapon, a cigarette poised between his lips.

When Liliana entered he sat back and assumed his usual distant expression. She looked at the gun.

'It's time?'

He nodded. A car drew up outside and he filled up a backpack, popped on a trilby-shaped hat with three feathers in it and left.

The 'time' it transpired was that point in the autumn when *uccellini* were caught or shot. I had no idea what they were, but went about the day with the backdrop of gun shots coming from the hills.

It was a Saturday and we'd had most of the day off, but we hadn't ventured far from the village. Usually on days like these we'd help ourselves to leftovers. It was shortly after noon and we were doing just that when the place was filled with laughter and the sound of men's boots on the marble corridors. Manolo strode into the kitchen followed by three other men, one I recognised as an *operai* called Lancelotti.

A bag was laid on the table, a bottle of grappa came out and they set to drinking. Nonna almost floated in. She observed the bag and Manolo tipped the contents onto the table. *Uccellini* were small birds, anything that wasn't a quail; there was about thirty of them. Nonna glowed and I swear that she licked her lips.

That night we were invited to dine with the family, even Domenico was there. Liliana and Manolo had two children, Donata and Monica, whom by this point I knew quite well having spent my evening with them swapping English for Italian lessons. Several good bottles of wine appeared and, after a plate of pasta, a large platter arrived with the cooked *uccellini* wrapped in parchment. I took one and slowly unwrapped the paper, a glorious waft of juniper and garlic rose up.

As I looked around the table I realised that I was taking part in a ritual. Nonna was in seventh heaven as she chewed and sucked the aromatic flesh from these tiniest of birds. They were delicious. Manolo, who was several hours of grappa the worse for wear, took a thin metal skewer and picking up a bird made a hole in the skull. He sucked the brains out with relish and, with challenge in his eyes, handed the skewer to me. He had no idea that brain sautéed in butter had been one of Mother's favourite dishes and that sweetbreads or offal of any nature held no terror for me. I can't say it was the most exciting part of that day's culinary experience, but the herbs made it very palatable.

Our stay at Campo Tizzoro ended when the two Italian girls who had previously come up to serve the winter skiing trade and the factory lunches had written to say they were now free for the coming season. I think we might have argued the case for staying, but although I liked the place, it was small and had all of the gossipy downside of that. The men were circling and, as all were married, it was only a matter of time before something unpleasant occurred. I'd already had a couple of encounters that were unwelcome and I knew that time had really run out. Snow had begun to fall and the temperature plummeted, and I had already had my fill of washing the sheets in the stream that ran alongside the hotel: no detergent, just you, a flat rock and a stone. I didn't relish doing that in December.

After a miserably damp tour of Germany and the Netherlands, whose highlight had been the herrings that were sold on the streets of Amsterdam, I returned to Columbia Road. It was 14 November 1974, almost four months to the day since I had left. It was a relief to be enfolded in Mum's hug. Neighbours came out onto the street to see what all the noise and fuss was about as she was almost hysterically happy to see me. A ripple of laughter and applause ensued before doors were closed to let us get on with the homecoming. I'd given my parents an estimate of a date of my arrival, but the hovercraft had been grounded due to bad weather, and she'd feared the delay meant that we'd had another idea about extending our trip. I'd had no such intention.

My time at Campo Tizzoro had been unique. Never again would I be in an environment where everything was produced so locally. The meat was butchered down the valley, from where the milk also came. Fruit and vegetables, if not grown nearby, were all Italian. Wine came from Chianti or courtesy of Liliana's father, who made great vats of what was called *vino nero*, black wine, in his garden in Pistoia. It was like drinking alcoholic Ribena. Rabbits and wild boar roamed nearby and were shot for the table. It was, I came to realise, a culinary idyll of the type that intensive farming and the global movement of produce has all but eradicated.

The rest of the trip had widened my horizons, but in effect we had simply trodden a well-worn tourist path. By its end I knew that I didn't like living out of a suitcase and viewed travel for its own sake an irrelevance. I wasn't yet ready, though, to slot back into serious study or permanence, but it was now a cold and wet November and I needed a job.

Chapter 11

Back to Work

I had never wondered what lay behind the neon lights of Piccadilly Circus, had never before observed the eyelet-like windows that looked out onto the statue of Eros. Even though Dad had often taken me to the cartoon cinema, which had sat on the corner of Shaftesbury Avenue. I remembered this as I stood looking up at the enormous red Coca-Cola sign at 'the Dilly'. From when I was five years old we had occupied our Saturday mornings either here with Looney Tunes and *Tom and Jerry* or at the Odeon cinema on Hackney Road with the latest children's showing of a film. These were frequently Westerns, which had the boys howling and squawking and the girls quiet and bored. Many years later when I went to Monument Valley I was surprised to find that the landscape, that I had assumed to be cut-out cardboard sets for the films, was real.

Dad and I had seen *Ben-Hur* at the suitably apt Coliseum Cinema on St Martin's Lane. The chariots had seemed to leap out of the screen at you and for a brief moment I'd had a childlike crush on Charlton Heston.

I now entered the battered door, which I must have walked past a thousand times before without ever noticing it. In front of me was a decrepit set of stairs illuminated by the constant glimmer from the neon signs which flashed through the filthy windows of the stairwell. I had an appointment with an agency that supplied temporary laboratory staff to institutions. It seemed an unlikely place for such an organisation, but there was no doubting the address.

The office was, in keeping with the staircase, small and unkempt. I sat on a chair and waited while a shy, softly spoken African woman was interviewed by an imperious blonde with cut-glass diction and steely grey eyes. It was an odd place and money laundering came to mind, although I couldn't figure out who'd be using the service, nor how anyone could tolerate working amid the red flashing lights. It did have a W1 postcode, so I assumed something nefarious was afoot as I couldn't imagine the staff making a bean from the operation on display.

My turn came and the classy blonde looked through my CV. She had jobs aplenty she said out in the provinces, with accommodation if I wanted it. I didn't. I wanted any job as long as it was in central London, I wasn't fussy. My plan was to recoup some money and maybe find a place of my own to live.

The Royal Ear Nose and Throat Hospital to which she sent me was just down the road from the Royal Free, and if I had thought that the Free was antiquated, the RENT made me think again. Yet as with the Free and its reputation in respect to disorders of the liver, RENT was world renowned for treatment of cancers of the thorax. Aged and dilapidated buildings it seemed did not equate with poor service. The first time I entered the lab I was confronted by the sight of a woman, her eyes closed, sitting at a microscope. Beside her a cassette player was playing an aria from an opera which I came to know well; it was *Orfeo ed Euridice* by Gluck, sung by Kathleen Ferrier. At a bench just by the door sat a young man who was performing a crossmatch. He had bouncing blond curls, piercing blue eyes and a wry smile. He nodded towards the woman, who was seemingly in a music-induced trance and raised his eyebrows.

'Penny!' he called out.

She opened her eyes, slowly came back from her reverie, and switched the player off.

Penny Laver was a relative of Rod Laver, the Australian tennis star, and she loved opera, no she adored it, and she wanted everybody else to embrace it too. She was slender, tall and wore cravats. I soon learned that she had no need to work, but for some reason had garnered a qualification in science, sufficient to allow her to 'run' the haematology and blood transfusion lab at RENT. It was the kind of place where the senior hospital managers could do what they liked. The prevailing opinion was that lab staff were ten a penny and after a couple of weeks' training anyone could do anything. It was frankly criminal, but the place was far from unique in those days.

She introduced the young man as Robert, and then began looking at slides while he showed me around. He was almost six feet tall and very slender, with pale freckled skin and a friendly manner. I warmed to him instantly. The equipment looked like it had come from a bring-and-buy sale and was so old as to almost be irreparable. Much was done by hand, which was fine as I could easily handle that. Blood transfusion was one bench in the room. In the corridor outside, when he was showing me the cloakroom, I asked him about the music.

'She's bats in the belfry about opera. I wear ear plugs when she gets into Wagner.'

It was an art form I had yet to dabble in, but it transpired that Robert knew quite a lot about opera. He knew a lot about a lot of things. He spoke Japanese, which was unheard of for a Westerner. He'd had a position in a Japanese bank, or so he said. Rob was a couple of years older than me and we were destined to be friends from the start. Neither of us fitted into the wider society and were attracted to one another's difference.

He presented himself as a clown but was far from stupid. He was a wild card with a heart, a chancer who would use you and he was utterly fascinating. Over the years of our association I came to realise that I used him too. In many respects I lived a vicarious life through him. I would often call his courage stupidity, his hedonism disgraceful, but he was like a drug and represented a kind of freedom I wanted but was too afraid to reach out for.

He didn't do rules and he broke the law when he felt like it. I first observed this when we went out to bleed the patients just before Christmas 1974.

The RENT pioneered many operations and was surgically at the forefront of facial reconstruction post-cancer therapy. Cancers of the larynx were treated with radiation with some success too. One of the failures was a man called Mr Holt whom I had bled a couple of times. He was a small elderly man whose cancer had spread just about every-where. He'd gone from believing he'd be cured to knowing he would not. He'd had a laryngectomy and couldn't speak, but could communicate by writing or nodding.

When we entered his room, just before Christmas, his eyes lit up. Rob grabbed his hand as I busied myself with the pointless task of taking yet more blood from his poor pinpricked arms.

He had a feeding tube, from which Rob removed the stopper and held it out to me. I was bemused.

'Just hold it here,' he said, indicating the height. He then popped a funnel into the tube, placed three plastic cups on the bedside table and with a flourish took a bottle of whisky from his white coat pocket.

'Single malt, just as you asked,' he said, winking at Mr Holt.

'Rob!'

He stared at me and poured measures into our cups.

'With or without?'

Mr Holt nodded and Rob poured some water in each cup, gave one to me and poured a small shot into the feeding tube.

'Cheers.'

Mr Holt sighed and closed his eyes in contentment. Rob chatted away amiably, and every once in a while the patient nodded or smiled at something he said. When he wanted more drink, Rob topped him up. By the time we had to leave Mr Holt was slumbering peacefully having consumed about half a bottle.

'You might have killed him,' I said, as we stood on the stairwell.

'And?'

'What do you mean, "and"?'

'Look, I've known him since he came walking in all full of hope of defeating it. To see him end up like this . . . He asked me for the booze.'

'It's not our job to play God.'

'Oh get off your high horse. He's Scottish, he wanted a whisky, big deal.'

I crossed my arms.

'All right, he wants to die before Christmas, give his family a break. He's had enough, they've had enough. He wanted something normal in what's left of his days.'

'And if he does die because of the drink?'

'He's dying anyway, isn't he? Lin are you going to tell on me?'

I shook my head. He was right. The man was on so much morphine already it was simply a matter of time.

It transpired that Rob wasn't the only one close to me who was challenging convention at that time. Mum had continued to work in the rag trade but finally had enough of the bad conditions and the boss's wife, who had a mouth the size of the Blackwall Tunnel out of which 'nothing good ever came'. Dad's pensions didn't add up to much, and as Mum was too young for her state benefit, it was time for a career change.

Reed employment bureau had an office at Liverpool Street station. Mum had never touched a typewriter nor run a switchboard, yet without a reference landed a job with a management company nearby run by a man with a hyphenated name but an easy to remember first name of Jonnie.

Whatever the nature of Jonnie's work was, we never really understood, or Mother never divulged it. Mum was ostensibly there to run the small telephone exchange and be what I imagine was a general dogsbody, but somehow she became much more than that. Her first foray into the mores of the switchboard was on her first day. Left to tend the beast over lunch she simply connected lights as she saw fit.

Jonnie had rushed out of his office.

'You've just connected me to my brother-in-law whom I haven't spoken to in months!' he shouted.

Mother had the best put-down looks and collection of one-liners on the market. 'Expect you had a nice chat then?'

Jonnie retreated a little. 'Who are you?'

'Mrs Wilkinson.'

A couple of days later she smashed one of his priceless tea cups which was coated in gold leaf. Jonnie was outraged, but she calmly told him that you should never use anything that you couldn't bear to be broken. At this point she was rather inelegantly gluing the cup back together.

'Nice white bone china's what you need. Easy to replace.'

'Oh really?'

Her world was street markets, his Harrods. It wasn't that we never visited up-market emporiums, we just never bought anything which wasn't in a sale.

'Yes. Something not so fine, I'd say,' she continued.

'All right.'

This may have been how it began. Perhaps she reminded him of his nanny, for sure she cannot have been like his mother who apparently had been all cut-glass syllables and wore couture by Chanel. Maybe he just saw the humour in Mum coupled with her peculiar code of honour. Whatever it was, within a short while she had not only taught herself how to run the switchboard, but how to repair the photo-copier and a variety of machines that were in residence. She mined Dad's supply of tools from his time in the navy to aid her task of becoming the lynchpin at work. Her alleged typing skills were laid bare for the lie that it was but she soldiered on and was soon typing Jonnie's letters, the kind of which I imagine were for their eyes only.

Soon she was bombing around town in taxis delivering large brown paper envelopes stuffed with cash to lords, MPs and ambassadors. The first time she did this was to a lord who had a flat behind Westminster Abbey.

'Some lord I'd say. You should have seen the place. Needed a good dust if you ask me and the carpets were all but threadbare.'

I imagined that these were almost certainly some very expensive, woven silk heirlooms.

'And the stairs, steep and rickety. He's an old codger, I wonder he doesn't break his neck.'

She called him Lord Smith, but I always had doubts as to the truth of that. Whoever he was he took to Mother, who early on registered her dislike of lapsang souchong, his preferred tea. Over the fairly lengthy period of their associa-tion she retrained him to give her a cup of Typhoo when she visited. She liked him, that was certain. He was the only one of her 'clients' she ever really talked about.

During her time as courier extraordinaire, if the delivery was in an afternoon she insisted on taking her shopping with her so that she could go straight home afterwards. She bought her fruit and vegetables in Whitecross Street Market which was near to her office on Moorgate.

One day she was sent to the Brazilian Embassy in Mayfair.

'The doors opened automatically and I walked in. There I was standing on top of a flight of stairs that went down to a white marble lobby. In fact, everything was white marble. I've seen some places, but it was really gorgeous, and clean. A way in the distance was a mahogany desk and at it sat a beautiful young man with jet-black hair. I put my shopping bags down and a cauliflower fell off the top, we both watched as it rolled down the stairs to stop halfway between me and him.'

He'd looked surprised but being a gentleman he had sauntered over to scoop up the offending vegetable. He met Mother on her way down the stairs. She gave him a brown paper envelope and he returned the now-bruised cauliflower.

'Do you know, he had no idea how to cook it. Don't have them in Brazil, apparently.'

My brother Tony and I were horrified that she might get caught; the legality of it was beside the point to us. We sat her down one night and begged her to stop.

'It's all right. Who's going to suspect me of anything?'

It may have been true, but this was a different league to when she had sold butter that had been 'lifted' from a shop; or when she and Dad had bought alcohol for Christmas from a consignment stolen from a lorry on the M1. Or even when she'd had a dining room suite and sideboard stolen to specification for her by an 'uncle' I'd never met before and never saw again.

'Mum, what are you actually up to?' I asked.

'I don't ask.'

'Look,' Tony said. 'He's not our kind of people. You must see that. If you get caught you'll be on your own.'

She refused to engage and the situation continued as we waited for her to be discovered.

Her greatest pleasure was buying clothes for Jonnie's mistress, Melissa. Apparently Melissa had visited work dressed for a night out on the tiles and Jonnie had noticed Mum's moue at the apparel she wore. The next day he asked Mum what she would suggest might suit Melissa.

Having worked in sweat shops on slave money, how it must have delighted her to be able to terrorise Bond Street. She knew exactly where the clothes were made, and by women exactly like her. It must have been a bit like the scene in the movie *Pretty Woman* where the boutique assistants look down their noses at Julia Roberts's character. Then, one call to Jonnie by the staff and they were eating out of Mum's hand. She had exquisite taste and a real eye for clothes and what suited people.

Unfortunately, Jonnie died 'on the job' with Melissa, and although the company would have kept Mum on, she decided to cut her losses. Typically, she made nothing over and above her salary for this adventure into politics and corruption. She remained tight lipped about it until her dying day, and I suspect it was just as well none of us really knew what she had been up to. Only once did she let it slip that she had purchased a question in the House of Commons on Jonnie's behalf. If my memory serves me correctly it was about a planning decision on a housing development. Not terribly exciting or sexy, but no doubt very profitable. What Jonnie had been paying the Brazilian ambassador for we never knew.

Chapter 12

Friends and Others

Between the ages of nineteen and thirty-three there were few significant people in my life; the most significant of these was Jenny, and I find writing about her difficult. I had thought that I could include her only fleetingly in this memoir, that she could appear on the pages as a ghostly figure loitering in the background, insubstantial and ill defined. There, but not. I wanted to spare her the embarrassment that our relationship became to her. The thought of her reading this work and recognising herself within it is hard to countenance even all of these years later. But not to mention her at all would be an act of betrayal about someone who was there during my journey from confused young adult to maturity. One thing knowing her, and leaving her, taught me is that without truth and honesty in its execution any life, or relationship, is bound to fail.

I'd had sex with men, as had she, but the backdrop was that we were THE relationship. One to which we would always return. Within it was security and companionship, but we never talked about the future or why we stayed together. We should have done; we should have talked about many things, but when a conversation became difficult she became silent and morose, so I learned to leave well alone. In the end, I came to feel that my needs were never paramount to her; I was second best in all respects. Yet for years I was happy to drift along, letting her drive our lives.

Once we came back from our travels we'd decided to live together and firstly rented a flat, which was the top floor of a small house in Tottenham. It was owned by a skinflint of an older landlady who lived nearby. Downstairs were a bunch of students with whom we had no interaction. The place was ghastly but served to stamp my independence while living in London. Dad roused himself to come over and put up shelves in the kitchen, which I painted spearmint green and purple, and Irene, Jen's mother, found us an unwanted stray cat and tried to become our cleaning lady, something I resisted.

Irene was still living with her husband and had her own household to run, so handed back the keys to our place without a fight. Having grown up with Alice and Clara in a house to which all areas were open, I needed something of my own. One of Alice's traits as she had aged had been to go through our cupboards and drawers. I had often found her at this task on coming in from school. She always had an excuse, but I knew they were old lady's lies. What she was looking for I have no idea.

Renting was money badly spent and by the age of twenty-three, courtesy of Jen's dad who stood as guarantor, I was on the housing ladder. We had sat dumbstruck in the Halifax Building Society as we were informed that they did not grant women a mortgage unless supported by a professional male. Pure discrimination of course. This was 1975 not 1875, but we went through the motions and at an interest rate of 15 per cent and for £12,500 we became the owners of a two bedroom, purpose-built ground floor flat near Bruce Grove railway station in Tottenham. The five years that we lived there was a period of studying and consolidating our careers. We had few friends, and those that we did have were mine, all of them met through work. Our neighbours were nice enough, but disinterested in socialising and, family apart, it became an isolated existence. Having grown up in a closely knit community, I struggled with this aspect of life. It wasn't that everybody on Columbia Road had been my friend, but I had understood the jigsaw of the place, knew where the fault lines were and how to avoid them. Here there seemed no warmth, no desire by the inhabitants to be either pleasant or friendly. It was an achingly anonymous experience.

I had hoped that, with the purchase of the flat, our relationship might develop. I knew that what I wanted from her was far more than I had, and I reasoned that if she had wanted a permanent man she would have found one by now. Yet, she never gave out any signals that it was anything other than a friendship and owning a flat simply a good investment. Other people seemed to view it as such, well at least to our faces. Lesbianism was absent from the public eye, or debate, in every way possible. If you didn't suspect you might be inclined that way, you need never have known it existed. Gay's the Word Bookshop didn't open until 1979 and the Greenham Common camp, which brought women of all persuasions to the public eye, was similarly in the future. Publications such as *Time Out* were unique in having gay listings, but from which women were almost absent. Classic French Literature of the mid- to late twentieth century were your best recourse for depictions of same sex love, but the 1973 publication of *Portrait of a Marriage* was hardly a book to have you heading towards the Sapphic bedsheets.

In 1975, although *The Naked Civil Servant* film of Quentin Crisp's memoirs promoted widespread and open debate, men were still being sacked and murdered for being gay.

One summer's day that year, when I was working at the RENT, I came in to find Rob sprucing himself up in the hand basin in the laboratory. I noticed he had grass in his hair and made some flippant comment about him having slept in Hyde Park. He had. Luckily Penny wasn't due in so we could talk freely. I can still remember the fear in his eyes as he confessed his sexuality.

'What would you say if I told you I might be gay?'

'I'd say I wasn't surprised,' I found myself saying.

Our friendship had not wandered into anything so personal before. We'd gone to pubs and restaurants, concerts and movies, and talked about art, music and Shirley Bassey, whom we both adored and, along with my parents, had seen at the Albert Hall.

Of course the evening before his confession he'd picked someone up and had sex with them in the park, but that was not the reason that he'd slept there. His family had thrown him out because the revelation of his sexuality was the last straw.

'What do you mean last straw?'

He had the grace at least to try and look sheepish as he

told me that a year before, having been bored by working, he'd falsified his father's signature on a cheque and took money from his bank account and had fled to the Continent. His father had informed the police, and on his penniless return to the UK Rob had been arrested. The deal between his father and himself had been that he would work to repay the debt or face jail. Of course, going back to his original job as a lowly junior technician was no longer an option, so he had found a position at the RENT where not too many questions were asked. Given our salaries, it was unlikely that he'd pay the debt off any time soon. As with everything else he had his own take on matters.

'He's got the money holed up in the bank. It's not as if he'll ever enjoy it.'

I did point out that it was his father's money to do with, or not, as he wished.

'They're all so bloody banal.'

How his family had found out about his sexuality he never revealed. I imagined all sorts of lurid scenarios but he'd probably just told them in a fit of pique. I doubt I have ever met anyone else who so profoundly disliked coming from what he described as the 'lower middle classes'.

During that long day at work, and longer evening in a pub, he told me about his travels. He was unabashed as he revealed that he'd been part of a group of young men who had serviced both one another and an ageing contessa who had lived in the south of France. It all sounded like a Somerset Maugham novel and I told him so, my scepticism palpable. He became emotional when he told me that she had died, that he'd become fond of her.

'I find that difficult to accept,' I said into my wine glass.

'She was intoxicating, such a free person. Did exactly what she wanted and took the consequences.'

I continued to disbelieve him until one day, when he had his own place, he showed me the white leather suit she'd had made for him. It was unlike anything I had ever seen and undoubtedly cost more than I could imagine. It was all he had left of her and he would never sell it. The contessa aside, he suffered from the delusion that he was born for better things and was determined to have them no matter what. From time to time he had money and I suspect, although do not know, that he sold sexual favours to feed his love of flamboyant clothes and a hedonistic lifestyle.

He wandered off into the night and ended up goodness knows where.

RENT aside, I had a succession of jobs in science that are best forgotten, but in 1976 I went to work at the Westminster Hospital. It was here that I met another of the people who would influence my life. The building itself was nothing like as ancient as many of the others I had worked in, but the laboratory was in an airless, windowless basement. Being the UK there was no air conditioning, which was fine most of the time as the summer temperature seldom soared and we were insulated from any of the sun's rays. However, the equipment itself generated heat and 1976 saw one of the hottest summers on record. For over a fortnight the daytime temperature exceeded 30°C and the lab became a hot house.

The machine on which we did the blood counts went way off scale. Every morning on start-up we'd run a series of standards through the system. Now the readings were meaningless. The fluid in which the samples were suspended during their passage through the analyser was so warm that the red cells were swelling and some were bursting. The recommended maximum temperature for efficient operation was 18°C; when we tested it the fluid hovered at 29.

We had two options, shut down and ship samples elsewhere or be creative. As other labs were reporting similar, if not such acute, problems, we opted for option two. I went out and purchased as much ice as I could, somebody found a large plastic container, and we stood the Isoton fluid container in a bath of crushed ice. Of course we couldn't let the temperature go too low or the cells would be equally affected and shrink as to be undetectable, so we took it in turns to check the temperature and lift the fluid from the ice as needed. We soon began making our own ice, as supplies had run out as everyone was buying it. Over the weeks, we refined our technique so that by the time the thunderstorms came and the temperature reverted to normal we had it cracked.

When I say we, it was primarily myself and a woman called Faye. She was older than me by thirteen years and had joined the lab soon after me as a senior technician. She'd been working at the prestigious Johns Hopkins Hospital in the US, where she and her husband had been living for a few years. Faye's attitude to life lay somewhere between that of Rob and Jenny. Faye wanted excitement and to sit outside of the mould of English middle-class life, but with the comfort a safety net. Rob hated the thought of conformity in any form and Jenny wanted the cocoon of convention. I never knew if Faye was different because she had been born in India, where she'd had a privileged late Raj existence along with servants and an ayah. Whatever the reason, she was unusual.

Physically she was small, dark haired and had a low-timbre voice which was intoxicating, and I found her attractive. She had married young and her husband, Ron, was a nice man of no great pretensions. They had met through work and at first glance seemed an ill-matched couple. It was obvious that it was she who drove the desire to travel the world; without her I doubt he would have left London. Latterly I came to appreciate that Ron was the safety net she needed and that she used him as her beard to the world. Whenever her activities threatened to spill out of the boxes in which she had hidden them, Faye would scuttle back to him, pull up the portcullis and wait until the coast was clear. Or until she deigned it time for another adventure.

She and I became firm friends and she and Rob got on really well; two eccentrics together, I thought. I wondered if it was from him that she got the information about the SM club she began to frequent in the West End.

'Can I tell you a secret?' she said, as we sat over lunch in the local Italian we used.

Why not? I thought. I'll just add it to my store.

Her eyes sparkled with devilment as she told me of her most recent escapade. I could see a narrow alley in Soho, a urine-sodden doorway and stairs down into a basement bar. It was called Stallions and some years later I visited it, although not on the SM night. Then a cloying smell of sweat, poppers and desire pervaded the air, but from her description it had been exactly the same in 1976. She described a series of rooms kitted out for the practice of varying degrees of consensual torture.

'They were all but naked,' she said with relish. 'Room after room of people doing indescribable things to one another.' She seemed in seventh heaven, although she insisted she hadn't got involved in any of the scenes.

'Was it a gay place?' I felt I had to ask.

She shook her head. Apparently there were all sorts there.

'I sat at the bar and had a lovely chat about mending washing machines with a chubby chap who was wearing a leather studded G-string.'

The image was far from appealing but served to paint a peculiarly English picture of sadomasochism.

'What does Ron say?'

She shrugged; as she went on the nights that he was on call, he need never know. She hinted that he might find it a turn on should she tell him.

'So take him along,' I suggested.

No. I could see in her eyes that wasn't the game, although I didn't fall into what that game was until 1984.

On my way home that night, I wondered if I should go to the club with her. If she had the ability to step out of her box, then why not me? Weighing up the pros and cons as to whether I would find it exciting or tawdry, I decided to see what Faye's progress might be before deciding. She went a few times more, but the tales remained the same, even down to the washing machine man. Unless she was going to indulge it became a static experience; SM is a game for two or more, after all.

Throughout the rest of my stay the Westminster I kept my head down and studied as hard as I could, and my time there passed well enough. Scientifically speaking, it was an interesting place to be. The Westminster Children's Hospital had as a patient Anthony Nolan, a young boy with a rare disorder called Wiskott-Aldrich syndrome which is a blend of immunodeficiency and a low platelet count and is life threatening. In 1976 Anthony was five years old and his redoubtable mother, Shirley, had already established the register in his name to find a suitable donor for a bone marrow transplant, which was the only prospect he had of surviving.

Shirley was a presence in the laboratory from time to time, as was Anthony. She was an energetic, driven woman who has done great good for the world, but sadly not for her son who died in 1979 without a suitable donor having been found. The charity she founded continues, however, and has half a million donors on its books.

It's strange to think that the origins of a major branch of scientific research began with a young medic called John Barrett who worked in a miniscule space just off the main laboratory. With a range of Heath Robinson equipment and no money, he laid the foundations of stem cell research. I often sat and worked with him as he ploughed his way through the challenge of fulfilling his ideas which, at that time, were seen by some as nonsensical. Today he runs a major unit in the US which continues the work begun in that airless, dark basement.

Apart from meeting Faye, Westminster wasn't a place that had a big impact on me. But there were a couple of events which stick in the memory as notable. One was when, due to staff sickness, I was the most senior person in the laboratory and so took charge, only to be challenged by a Nigerian male technician who would not take orders from a woman. He had the dual disadvantages of being very short and not very bright, so no matter how loudly he screamed the outcome was always certain. I had him marched out of the place by a porter and needless to say he only reappeared to be sacked by the senior management.

The other was both sad and funny. David was a lovely, anaemic-looking, very devout Jewish doctor who had diabetes. He lived at home in Golders Green with his mother and brought his food in from home. He was a kindly man who would do nobody harm; he spoke just above a whisper and the patients loved him. It was the time of the annual laboratory inspection by the powers that be. We had scrubbed and buffed the place, and now sat gainfully employed at our work spaces awaiting the arrival of the dignitaries. I was staring down a microscope when a size twelve shoe appeared on the bench in front of me. I looked up to see David red faced and smiling. He took off his white coat, grabbed his braces, snapped them, and crowed like a cockerel. He then proceeded to strut his stuff in what can only be described as a bump and grind rendition of 'I'm a Yankee Doodle Dandy', delivered at the very top of his lungs.

Faye shot in from the corridor. 'They'll be here in five minutes,' she gasped, as we stood and watched the cabaret.

'Start them somewhere else,' I said.

Somehow we bundled David into the coffee room, closed the door and tried to calm him.

I sat on his chest and various others of us restrained different bits of him as he thrashed around violently. Someone stuffed a gag in his mouth.

'He's having a hypo,' another of the medics said.

We attempted to pour a sugar solution down his throat. Poor chap, he had a moment of clarity and horror before lapsing into a semi-comatose state. I grabbed a phone and called Casualty. By the time the inspectors had arrived we were all in place and working and David was in A&E.

In those days, insulin batches varied widely. We found out later that he'd just got a new batch of insulin and he'd fallen victim to that.

I managed to pass the written part of my haematology fellowship exam for the Medical Laboratory Sciences Institute but failed the viva. For such a garrulous person, I was poor at thinking on my feet. I had all of the knowledge but if confronted with direct questions I clammed up.

'Have a shot of something,' Dad said, as I was preparing to go to the repeat viva. I was at home at Columbia Road as the examination was going to take place at the London Hospital. I'd thought that a bit of parental boosting wouldn't go amiss before the twenty-minute walk there. I demurred; turning up with booze on my breath was not a good idea, I thought. However, by the time I got to Whitechapel Road I was shaking. I went into the Grave Maurice, the hospital pub, and ordered a double brandy. Sitting in a corner like a lonely old alcoholic I studied my notes.

I needn't have worried as, the viva being immediately after lunch, my examiners were blotto and the session turned into a wander down memory lane. One was a chief medical laboratory scientist and the other a consultant haematologist with whom I had worked while at the London Hospital in 1973. There was some science involved, but not as much as was probably required, and luckily they homed in on thalassaemia, known parochially as Mediterranean anaemia, which was one of my favoured areas of study.

I passed, and in January 1977 I took up a post as a senior in charge of the haemophilia centre of University College Hospital. I had studied the subject of coagulation to the appropriate level and, although I wouldn't have said it was my preferred option to take forward as a speciality, I was a pragmatist. Senior positions in London weren't ten a penny and I was ambitious both to earn a greater salary and to go as far as I could in the profession.

Chapter 13

Diagnosis

On the first Wednesday in my new post I met William Dumbelton. I'd crossed over with Peter, the person vacating the position I had just been promoted to, who was moving back to Wales. He'd given me the lowdown on the major cases of bleeding disorders which were on the books, and William was one of those. He was a classic case of haemophilia with much of the familial baggage that came with it. Born in 1942, the shock of his condition meant that his parents refused to have another child. His mother in particular was riddled with guilt as the disorder is carried on the X chromosome, so it came from her. The bleeds into his joints during his childhood had been major and he used crutches to move around. He had an adapted car and held down a job at the Post Office.

Every week he would pick up the supply of cryoprecipitate that he needed to survive. Cryoprecipitate is produced when frozen human plasma from a blood donation is thawed slowly at just above freezing. The resultant clump of proteins included the Factor VIII that he lacked. When we first met he was very unsure about me, as he'd known Peter for a long while. Trust and confidence in the person handling your case is vital with long-term conditions. Luckily we hit it off, and although notionally cared for by medically quali- fied personnel, in effect it was I who handled most aspects of his prophylactic treatment.

He wanted to go onto a product which didn't mean that you had a freezer full of blood bags. They were dif- ficult to handle, split regularly when they were thawed out in warm water and, if you didn't notice a split, carried the risk of injecting yourself with contaminated product.

Of course the difficulty was money. These better prod- ucts were not made in sufficient quantity by the Blood Transfusion Service to supply all of the country's needs and as a centre we had a meagre supply at best. William, however, was insistent, he wanted as near to a normal life as possible, and who could blame him. Eventually, I persuaded the departmental head to buy it for him from a commercial supplier. It turned out to be a pyrrhic victory.

William was delighted. It meant he didn't have to come in as often as he could store the Factor VIII in a fridge in small vials. The injections were small and the solution, when the freeze-dried product dissolved, was clear and easy to handle. There was little chance of the injection lines blocking up as before causing massive bruising to his arms. From time to time he had a bleed that he couldn't handle at home and was admitted to the hospital.

In those days we worked on percentages of normal as a range. Factor VIII level was in the range of between 50 and 150, William had 0.1 which was almost undetectable.

Performing coagulation tests is one of the most labour- intensive specialities in medical sciences. Some routine tests can be performed using machines, but assays such as those for detecting haemophilia and associated disorders are fully hands-on procedures. The equipment is rudimentary, a water bath at body temperature, good quality test tubes and internationally calibrated standards and fresh reagents. And above all good eyesight.

Dilutions of standard and patient plasma are made in deficient plasma, and after an incubation period a clot is induced by reintroducing the calcium which was removed when the blood sample was taken. Timing of the formation of the clot is done by eye and stopwatch, which given the multiple dilutions required is no easy feat, but when timed and staggered correctly I was able to handle four stopwatches at once. The times are linear for the standard but depending on the level of the patient's factor theirs can be any shape, or none. From this the levels are calculated. Gauging clot formation by eye requires skill and experience, for in people deficient the clots can be oddly ethereal, resembling a swirling mass of white fibrils which never fully clump.

All of this William lived in ignorance of; as long as he could live his life he was happy. Soon after he got the new product William took the step of getting married to a work colleague at the Post Office. He brought Linda in to meet me, ostensibly so that if he were sick she would know from whom to get his Factor VIII. She looked so young and was so incredibly happy and in love. William, Bill by now, was a good raconteur and storyteller who hid his disorder from the world, and the accompanying depression that it brought with it from time to time. I hoped that she knew what might lie ahead of her.

*

The job fascinated me. Apart from supporting people like William, it involved running the anticoagulant clinic and diagnosing an array of disorders. As UCH was the first major hospital stop on the way from Heathrow Airport, we saw a fair share of both health tourism and truly sick people who had come to London seeking help.

I worked at UCH for nine years, and in that time saw some interesting and bizarre cases. My training had been adequate, but had not prepared me for the range of issues that came to my door. I spent many a night after work in the medical school library poring over text books of obscure cases, looking for something that might resemble the ones currently on our books. Slowly I began to develop a repu-tation as someone you sent patients to if a diagnosis was difficult, or seemed frankly impossible. I have to say that sadly the medics, bar one, were not of much use.

The main thrust of the department was the diagnosis and treatment of thalassaemia and various leukaemias. Coagulation was a distant cousin to their interests and I was pretty much left on my own. I had long lost the fear that had seen me sleepless when I'd performed my first crossmatch. I knew that I could trust myself to dig deeply until a diagnosis was sound.

One of the straight from Heathrow to hospital cases was a Mr Muktar from somewhere on the Arabian Peninsula. He was a farmer on whose land oil had been discovered, but his newly found affluence was no short route to happiness.

Shortly after the discovery of his pot of gold he'd come down with a flu-type virus, soon his joints were swollen and he could no longer walk. Nose bleeds were an indication that his clotting system was under stress. Rudimentary tests had excluded septicaemia and seemingly a clotting disorder was not indicated. On arrival he was admitted to the private patients' wing where I went and bled him. A translator was present and I quizzed him about his health and his family. There was nothing untoward except the viral-type illness.

His clotting screen was just off normal, not enough to account for his condition, so I assayed everything and found that he had developed antibodies to his own Factor VIII. On paper he had sufficient, but in fact it was coated with these antibodies and was useless. It could not be activated. No amount of injected product helped, as it was similarly neutralised and only served to fuel the antibody production.

Poor man, he was in bed for nine months wasting away. He appeared to have no family, I never saw anyone visit him. It was a lonely, terrifying existence.

Finally, the decision was made to inject immunosuppressive drugs of the kind used in treating transplant patients to halt rejection. It was risky at best, but he was dying before our eyes. By now he spoke enough English and understood the proposition.

'It may kill me?'

I nodded. He shrugged and tears filled his eyes, as they did mine after I left his room. He was injected and we waited, and waited and waited. His parameters didn't shift.

One typically wet and windy London day, I went into his room and he was standing by the window. He turned and beamed the biggest smile I have ever seen and walked towards me.

'Gone, all gone,' he said showing me his knees which were a normal size. His parameters were completely normal as the clone of cells producing the antibodies appeared to have been switched off.

On the way to seeing Mr Muktar that day, I'd passed the room which housed a Bantu prince who was awaiting treatment for a hernia. His Highness discounted the bathroom and instead doused himself with bowls of warm water in the middle of his bedroom. The sister in-charge was berating him yet again for ruining her floor, when the doors to the goods lift which sat directly opposite his room opened and a fully sedated panda on a trolley was wheeled along the corridor. The prince on seeing this fainted away, and thereafter may have been persuaded to take his ablutions in the English style.

The panda had colic. From time to time the London Zoo used facilities in the private wing theatre to examine their patients. The only time I was disturbed by this was when I saw a tiger pass by in a similar state of somnolence, but I never heard that anything ever went awry. Soon afterwards the zoo built its own operating theatre and laboratory, which was a blessing. I had no idea of normal parameters on the range of animal samples I was sometimes asked to analyse. I never did find a normal range for clotting in camel blood.

It was humans who occupied my days and some of my nights, as I continued to seek to diagnose obscure and surprising manifestations of the body. It was deeply satisfying on many levels. The detective nature of uncovering a key paper that cited a similar range of symptoms to those of one of our patients was intellectually thrilling. Even more so when there was no written evidence of such a case, and I was left with no option other than to devise and adapt diagnostic techniques to find out what was happening. Emotionally, of course, if I got it right and discovered the root cause of the disorder, I was elated.

'I am not mad, let's just begin with that.'

Evelyn was a beautiful twenty-eight-year-old woman, from a well-heeled background, who had done the rounds of the hospitals. She had been referred to me as a last-ditch attempt before she undertook, or was forced to undertake, psychiatric treatment. I looked at her referral form. SEB, Simple Easy Bruising – a catch-all phrase often translated in medic speak as hysterical woman syndrome.

'They say I am doing it to myself, why should I?'

The bruises were large and covered her arms, chest and back.

'I want to get married soon, but how can I, not like this?'

She also couldn't hold down a job as along with the bruising she was depressed and constantly tired and often could not get out of bed. I took a history alongside one of the medics, a male of about the same age as the patient.

'She's barking,' was his estimation, after the consultation.

But I agreed with Evelyn. It would have taken some talent to produce the bruises she exhibited. I gave her samples to the scientist who was on rotation through my section, David.

'Odd, look at this,' he said a few minutes later.

One of the screening tests we did is called a thrombin time, which directly activates fibrinogen, the final part of the clotting pathway causing it to form a clot. David showed me the test tube. The time it took to react was normal, but the clot was far from that. It was full of strands and not solid as it should be, resembling nothing less than a transparent spider's web. I did some further tests and re-bled her.

'I'm like a pincushion.'

'Sorry, Evelyn.'

'You found something?'

'Maybe.'

More library work and I discovered a few other cases of what I suspected she had.

I took a sample of her plasma to David Lane at the Charing Cross Hospital, who was the world expert on fibrinolysis. Faye was working there at the time, which was another reason for going over.

That afternoon when I was back at UCH, David Lane called me. He reckoned I'd taken the sample badly, the results were not believable. I knew that the sample was sound, but I sent Evelyn to him so that he could observe her first hand. My sample and the one he drew were in accord.

It transpired that Evelyn had a growth called a giant cell haemangioma, which was secreting a product which was tipping her clotting system into a constant state of activation. The tumour had to be detected and removed, otherwise her prognosis was poor. It took some finding, but was finally detected deep in the muscle of her upper arm.

'You will have a god-awful scar,' the surgeon had told her. Comforting, I thought.

'Will it cure me?' she asked, just before they wheeled her into surgery.

I had no idea whatsoever, not telling her until afterwards I had only found four other examples of such a syndrome in the literature. Some tumours had been so deep and invaginated with other tissues that they could not be fully excised. After the operation she did have a terrible scar, but the bruising, depression and tiredness disappeared. I have no doubt that in the future a good plastic surgeon would have disguised the scarring well enough.

'Not so barking was she?' I parried at the male medic, knowing he would continue in his arrogant self-serving fashion.

It never ceases to amaze me how poor the diagnosis of certain conditions remains. One of the most common clotting disorders is Von Willebrand disease, and it is something I saw a lot of. Discovered in 1926, the disorder is one where the adhesion of platelets and the promotion of coagulation is slowed due to a defect in the eponymous protein Von Willebrand factor. It is usually inherited, but sometimes not, and can be mild or life threatening. It was also a condition, like Evelyn's, which was frequently attributed to a psychiatric disorder, as one of the symptoms is bruising. Strangely, men with bruising never had the soubriquet of hysteria attributed to their lesions.

Claudia, like Evelyn, was referred for bruising and, like her, had been viewed as a bit of a basket case. It turned out her VWD was quite bad. It's a strange disorder: levels of the various parts of the molecule involved often have little bearing on the severity of the bleeding, and on paper she was a mild case.

The big no-no with it is aspirin, as that decreases platelet aggregation and she had taken a lot over the years. Claudia liked a good time and a drink and had noticed that she had nose bleeds after a night out. Of course she had taken aspirin for her hangovers.

Her diagnosis had not been difficult but she found it hard to adapt her lifestyle. The leveller was when during some rambunctious sex with her fiancé she fell out of bed and broke her arm. The tissue bleed involved with that was spectacular; even after she was infused with product, she was incapacitated for a long while. It bought her up short and thereafter her visits to me became infrequent. I know that she married and hoped for children. Eventually she moved to another part of England and I lost touch with her.

A positive diagnosis for a disorder that will be with you for life is never welcome. Most people approach the news with dismay, but most also adapt to the situation. At about the same time as I diagnosed Claudia, I had a male patient come to the department for the same reason, bruising. He was a short, trim man who was very agitated at being there.

'All I want is a minor operation. Why am I here?' I can still hear him saying. Stereotypes are just that, but the man was somewhat fey and I thought was almost certainly gay. His problem was gynaecomastia, the appearance of breast-like protuberances on a male. As far as one could see, these weren't vast and nothing to get exercised about, but it was his body and they made him feel inadequate, or so he said.

I doubt I have ever seen anyone as crestfallen as he at the diagnosis of VWD. It took an inordinate amount of explaining as to what it was and what he should avoid taking as medicine. He point-blank refused to believe the diagnosis.

Luckily it wasn't I who had to deny him treatment on the NHS for what was in effect a cosmetic operation of no urgent need. He stormed out of the clinic saying that he would get it done privately. I have a nasty feeling that somehow he would have had it done without such rigour being applied to his blood screens elsewhere. All that, rather than confront what was almost certainly an underlying psychological problem in relation to self-image. The capacity for us to ignore physical evidence that's in front of our eyes never ceased to amaze me. We humans are capable of great self-delusion.

Chapter 14

End of an Era

O ne evening, in late 1979, I came home to find the bed
outside of my flat. It was on wheels, had springs and
a mattress, and symbolised nothing less than the end of an
era. Its appearance meant that the unthinkable had happened, my parents had left Columbia Road.

I have often envied people who can up sticks and move on,
live seemingly anywhere, but I am not one of those. As much
as my parents, the house at 77 Columbia Road had been a
constant in my life, and now it was no longer my home.

What had brought the family to this point was all very
logical. Dad's arthritis had been progressing and the conditions in the house were still hovering at the level of the year
1900, so Tony and my sister-in-law, Maggie, arranged for
them to move to a council flat near to them in Hornchurch.
Mum had called me at work a month before and demanded
my presence. She was cold, clinical and brusque.

'I've been asking you to take the rest of your stuff away
for ages. It's now or never.'

'Why?'

'We are moving.'

'What!'

She went on to tell me about the flat, unconcerned that I wasn't listening to her.

'You can't go,' I said that evening in her kitchen, as she was packing up crockery.

'I most certainly can and I will.'

Her mood was strange, almost triumphant.

'But—'

'But what?'

'You can't leave; you have to be here. Dad?'

He looked at me and shrugged.

'Don't bother your father. It's all arranged. Up you go, sort your mess out.'

'No.'

'Linda, you are twenty-seven years old. Act it.'

I walked upstairs and sat on the put-you-up, which had been moved to my old room when I had taken my own bedroom suite to the flat. I looked at the bare room and realised that she had been denuding the house of excess furniture for some time. This decision was not new. I heard Dad's laboured walk and wheezy chest as he navigated the stairs. He sat beside me.

'You said you'd never leave.'

He held my hand and we sat in silence until his breathing calmed.

'Tony offered to put in a bathroom for us here, down-stairs even. Make me a bedroom with an en-suite; put heating in. But she'd have none of it.'

'You could have said yes.'

'I tried, but I don't have the fight left. She's always wanted to go. Besides, we'll be near the grandkids.'

I burst into tears.

'It's not far,' he continued.

'You don't believe that.'

He smiled. 'No, it's not the distance, is it?'

He belonged here more than I did. His grandparents had come from the next street. He'd always lived there. Columbia Road ran through his veins like the letters through Brighton rock. The street and the Sunday market were ours, strangers seldom wandered along its scruffy length. It may have been unprepossessing, but there was a kaleidoscope of life upon it of which we were a part. My life in that moment seemed distilled into two colours, the grey of Columbia Road and the vibrant red of the blood that I handled every day, and by which I earned my daily bread. Stark in contrast, but both of equal importance to me.

'Listen Lin, you've got your own life now. It's not here any more, is it?'

I wasn't going to admit how lonely I was in my new flat in Tottenham, that I had no life and few friends. I couldn't tell him how often I'd thought about coming home.

'Why go?' I asked. 'Really?'

He took a deep breath. 'Your mother has made a lot of sacrifices for me.'

'And it's her time to have what she wants?'

'It's not a story for me to tell.'

'Oh, don't tell me another bloody secret.'

I was to learn no more, a shutter came down, subject closed. He stood and looked down at me. For a long moment he said nothing, then his expression softened.

'One day, you know, people will discover this place and

you won't be able to buy a house here for love nor money,' he said softly.

'But we won't be here to see it?'

'No.'

I felt empty, as empty as I have ever felt. Empty and abandoned. I knew that I was being childish. It had hardly been a home full of laughter at times, but it had always been a part of me. I had an overwhelming sense that I was reneging on unfinished business which would now never be resolved.

The floor to ceiling cupboard that Mum wanted me to empty was packed with books and memorabilia of my younger self, and I began sifting through them. In the end I took just a few things. On my way out, I asked Mum where I would sleep when I came to visit them.

'On the floor, I suppose.'

I was taken aback by her harshness.

'What about the put-you-up?'

'What about it?'

'I can sleep on that.'

She actually narrowed her eyes, the first and last time I ever saw her do that. It was a brief window into her real feelings. To her, the house had been a place of hardship and sometimes servitude as she had struggled to support her own and my father's family. Hornchurch signalled liberation from the past and she wanted no extraneous baggage or responsibilities. I had chosen my own path and she was signalling exactly that. There would be no moving back in with Mum if things went wrong for me.

'No need for that any more. You want it?'

I didn't want it, but saying yes was a victory of sorts against her glacial demeanour. We agreed that Tony would deliver it some time soon. I called a cab to pick me up and, as I was loading it, Ginger Lil 'happened' by.

'Hear they are going?'

I was unable to speak.

'End of an era?'

'Dad's sick,' I managed.

'Well, they're like rats leaving a sinking ship if you ask me.'

'Lil, leave it alone, please.'

She saw my pain and with a grace I'd never have credited her with, patted me on the shoulder. 'See you again sometime.'

She walked the few doors along to where she lived. Her ginger hair glinted in the sunlight and the wood dust danced in the air. I looked at the old house once more and left.

A week later, I wheeled the put-you-up into the storage space beneath the stairs and locked the door both on it and the past life that it represented.

Several months later I found myself luxuriating in a black and gold bathroom in another part of town.

'You'd make a good bloke.'

Rob was lying on the bed as I wandered back in from the shower wearing one of his shirts. We were in the new flat that he was sharing with Bill, who was a floor walker at the Army and Navy Stores in Victoria and whose speciality was ladies' handbags.

'Really? And what would I do as a bloke?'

'Ah well, there's a story.'

There was always a story with Rob, who had reappeared in my life after an absence of a few months. I never asked where he had been, I guessed I most likely wouldn't like the answer he gave. It would have been drugs, sex and rock and roll, and I was still cautious about the first two. He knew everything about me; I hadn't told him about my fancying women, although of course he had guessed that too.

I was for the first time in my life really slender and I had small breasts, hence his comment. Rob was naked except a pair of underpants which did little to hide his interest.

'If you are going to say you fancy me you can sod off.'

I lay next to him and studied the decorated ceiling with its ornate plasterwork.

Bill had been a tenant at the flat for years. Older than Rob by many years, he'd invited him in to share the rent and, from time to time, much else besides. I don't know how they met, I never asked. The apartment was in Warwick Square in Pimlico and was a queen's delight, with a vast mirror in the lounge which Bill insisted that he'd purloined from the skip outside Judy Garland's apartment after she'd died. True or not, I loved the place with its outlandish gold-encrusted wallpaper in the lounge, the high ceilings and a record collection which featured just about every torch singer of note since recordings began.

'I mean it, if you would dress up as a bloke,' he hesitated, 'there's a real appetite out there.'

'For?'

'Oh, come on, Lin. You hang around with me, you can guess.'

'And who would I be entertaining?'

He rolled onto his stomach. 'You need never do anything. Just be there and talk.'

'Oh, really?'

Rob had moved on to what was to be one of many positions in a private laboratory, where of course he was the life and soul of the party and from which he obtained substances from both the pharmacy and others who worked there. He never told me about this, but Bill let it slip one day. I gathered that his entrée into some of the parties that he frequented was eased by his ability to supply.

'I don't do drugs,' I said.

'I know, and as far as I can see you don't do sex. What do you do for fun?'

I couldn't answer, he was right.

'Tempted?' Rob cooed at me and pulled me on top of him.

Of course I was. I loved my job but other than that things were difficult. I could only go on ignoring who I was for so long.

Jen and I had recently moved from the flat in Tottenham to a house in Barnet, again in north London. The service charges we had paid on the flat's leasehold had been reasonable, until the roof needed substantial work. We paid our share of what was going to be an ongoing expense and moved on. On balance, it seemed best to buy a freehold. That was what I told the world; the deeper truth was that I was having problems dealing with Jenny and her family, more precisely her mother.

I hadn't wanted to move so far out, as I saw it, but over the years Irene had suffered from increasingly poor mental health. She and her husband had parted company and she now lived alone in a flat. Some time before, despite my earlier success at curbing her, she had become our housekeeper and cleaner after all, appearing whenever she wished. Of course I felt sorry for her, but I felt as if my home wasn't mine. I had hoped that if we moved to Barnet, Irene wouldn't follow us due to her nervous disposition. But, lo, there was a direct bus from her flat, and now she was our gardener as well.

It wasn't working, I was depressed and the rows I had at home went nowhere. Seemingly, I shouldn't want my weekends to myself. Also, I'd begun dreaming about my great-aunt Clara. This always happened when I was stressed or upset, and I wanted those dreams to stop as they left me shaken and haunted.

All of this was compounded by the fact that I no longer had a bolthole. I had frequently gone home to Columbia Road at weekends, and sometimes during the week, for a dose of familial sanity. The familiarity of my old street had served to calm me, but going there was no longer an option.

Weighing it up, I thought that Rob's proposition might bring a welcome diversion to my sombre mood.

'Maybe I should take up rock-climbing,' I offered.

'Ha, ha. Well?'

'Tell me more.'

'No. Come along and see for yourself.'

I have to admit that I did look good in a dress suit. I kept the clothes he got for me at his place and we'd head off in a taxi to a central London location where he would be greeted by any one of a number of well-known faces. My role was to drift around making conversation, drinking wine and being sexually ambiguous. Sometimes I wore make-up, sometimes not.

'Drop your voice,' he said to me one night.

'Nope, this is as far as I go towards a baritone.'

'Please.'

I wouldn't and he was annoyed. I soon understood why when I met a very famous man who would have relished undressing me to discover a girl beneath the facade. Not that he would have had the opportunity.

This went on for a while, and I developed a reputation as quite exactly what I was never sure.

One night Rob was very nervous as we prepared to go out. He didn't do nervous and I wondered if he was taking drugs himself, something he always denied. Nevertheless, we went out as usual but to somewhere we had never been before, where it became obvious something was afoot. I was used to people drifting off in pairs or more to rooms and to reappear later. Of course I knew what was going on and turned a blind eye, just as long as I could float around enjoying myself. This night I was ushered into a room, a bedroom, to meet someone. I recognised her immediately. Like many at those parties her face was often in the press, but I'd had no idea of her proclivities. She was disappointed that I wouldn't play, but we passed time amicably enough over a few drinks, during which I discovered the price Rob had demanded for a few hours with me.

'If you ever change your mind Rob can get hold of me,' she said with apparent regret.

When I emerged he was hovering. I slapped him in front of his so-called friends and left. He chased me out onto the street.

'How dare you,' I said, assuming a strangely moral high ground.

He laughed and shook his head.

'You sold me, Rob. When were you going to tell me? Or were you going to just take the money and stay shtum?'

'Oh Miss Innocent, listen to yourself. Wandering around teasing the whole of London, what did you expect?'

'I am not for sale.'

'What are you then? You are too clever to be that stupid. Surely you knew there was going to be some kind of payback time?'

In truth, I had expected that nothing would happen. I had assumed it would continue until the pastime palled and I moved on. Of course, this was naive in the extreme and any fool would have known that; just not this fool.

Only I knew how tempted I had been. It would have been all too easy to slip into that world of apparent wealth and elegance. This was probably the time that I should have leapt and taken the chance to find out who I was. I was a nothing and a nobody to these people, so could probably have played in anonymity.

But I came from the East End and knew the reach of the criminal classes, what concrete boots were, and what happened if you fell into the Thames while wearing them. Fanciful as that may seem, I had no illusions as to the consequences that an unguarded comment about whom I had met might bring. Was my breeding holding me back from the hedonistic world of the 1970s? Of course it was, but that wasn't the whole story.

I grabbed a taxi and went home.

Chapter 15

Living and Learning

'Remember Janet?'

Jenny was uncharacteristically nursing a large gin when I got home from work. I did remember her, she was a technician who ran the satellite laboratory that the London had at Mile End Hospital. I'd always liked her as, like Faye, she was a bit off the wall and, like Faye, she was married to a man, Pete, who seemed the definition of pleasantly average. Jenny was now working at the London Hospital with Margaret Kenwright.

'She was riding that bloody enormous motorbike of hers when a lorry clipped the back of it and catapulted her through the railings of Bethnal Green Hospital.'

'Dead?'

'Worse.'

Seemingly, over the intervening years since I had left the London, the staff at the two laboratories had begun to rotate. The scientist who had got the request for blood from A&E had frozen when she realised who it was for, as they were close friends.

'It was chaos; the staff fell apart. Margaret did her Joan of Arc act and pulled them back together. She was incredibly harsh.'

'I imagine she's had to be over the years.'

Jenny, who was no wilting flower in the harshness depart-ment, always found my sticking up for Margaret tough to swallow.

Janet was so badly injured that nobody thought she would pull through. She had brain damage, smashed bones and muscles, her kidneys were affected and the scarring on her body awful. When she'd arrived at A&E they'd cut the clothes from her body but X-rayed her through her helmet, where the fracture was revealed.

'How'd they get the helmet off?' I asked.

'Christ knows. She's in a coma.'

I poured her another drink and went to cook dinner.

Over the next few months Janet slowly improved and, finally, she was sent home and we went to visit her. She lived in a standard Edwardian terraced house in Leyton and Pete let us in, looking tired and harassed. I'd met him only once or twice before at Christmas parties, but had hardly passed a word with the man. He was slight and blond-haired and attractive in a slightly feminine way.

Janet sat in a wheelchair in the lounge. Medical equipment was strewn everywhere and she was hooked up to a drain. A scar ran down the middle of her face, one eye had collapsed almost out of recognition and she was in constant pain. At some point in the near future, Jenny was going to have to tell her that she was going to lose her job. Janet was clinging on to the idea that she would improve enough to return. She adored her work and her colleagues but there was no way she would ever be able to perform the tasks required safely.

I wasn't there when the coup de grace was delivered, but it sent her into a spiral of acute depression. By now Pete was back at work and she was alone much of the time. I visited to find her desolate and suicidal.

'I keep looking at the wallpaper hoping it'll talk to me.'

I made some comment about Pete being there at night. She laughed with the one side of her face that still worked.

'He's into his scuba diving again. Can't blame him, who'd want to look at this.'

There was no adequate response. Because both of us knew and understood that the uplifting banter with which we talked to patients in distress was just that, banter. We sat in silence.

'I want to die, Lin. What's the point of it all?'

But the next time I saw her, which was some months later, she was walking with the aid of a stick. She'd got some help at a group counselling session and things slowly improved. Her car had been adapted in order that she could drive, and she was wearing brightly coloured clothes and seemed buoyant. She was in the throes of getting a set-tlement from the driver of the lorry that hit her. Seemingly it was all his fault, so financially things were on the up and losing her profession wasn't quite the blow it had seemed it might be. Over the next few months we became quite close and she invited me up to the Birmingham car show. I didn't drive, didn't really care about cars, but I went. She had a friend with her, a woman from the counselling group, called Chris. Janet was a real car enthusiast and dis-abled as she was dragged us around with obvious delight. At one point I thought she was going to spend a fortune on a sports car.

'Speed's not your friend, Jan.'

'Bugger that.'

Soon after that she came around to my place for a coffee.

'Remember when I was waiting for the wallpaper to talk back? Well, it wasn't just about the accident and Pete. I had some shit to deal with, stuff that's been bugging me for years. Having the time to think meant that I couldn't run away.'

She was sure, she said, that I would be all right with what she was about to tell me. She said that although she loved Pete, and she did, she'd always fancied women. Chris and she were now an item and she'd never been happier. I said nothing while she waited expectantly.

'And Pete?' I finally managed.

'I haven't told him yet.'

'You going to?'

'I have to. I want Chris to move in.'

It seemed so precipitous and emotionally dangerous. Chris had been with an abusive male partner, Janet through a horrendous physical trauma. I didn't know what to say.

'You seem shocked.'

'Is it wise?'

'Fuck wise, I should be dead. It's what I want.'

And get it she did, although not without some further trauma.

Within a few weeks Pete had moved out and Chris in. It was no love nest, however. They argued constantly, it seemed that the arguments fuelled the relationship.

Her house was often filled with women from Janet's increasing circle of lesbian contacts. Women from Australia and the US used her place as a base when they were in

Europe, and they all seemed to have slept with, or were sleeping with, one another. It was hard to believe the vitality that Janet exuded, given that her physical state was still poor. I admired her for her fight and the way she had carved a life for herself in such an unconventional manner.

However, I hadn't seen her for a good few months when the phone rang. She needed some help.

'I told Pete I want a divorce,' she said. 'He tried to kill himself.'

Even by Janet's standards this was high drama, and I was at a loss as to where I might fit into this equation.

'I wondered if you'd see him. Go out, like. He's very low and he likes you.'

'I hardly know the man.'

'Look, just go to the pictures, out for a meal please. He's in a bad way.'

'I'm no shrink.'

'But you are a good listener.'

'I am not, don't bullshit me, Janet.'

'Please. At least think about it.'

She gave me his work number and hung up.

Janet had said divorce was not something he'd countenanced, assuming that her sexuality was part of a reaction to her accident and that one day they might be together again. I figured there was no harm in calling him, as it seemed that he and I were in the same boat where being alone was concerned.

At that time, he was living in one room in a large house overlooking Wanstead Flats in Redbridge on the Essex borders. It was here that the physical side of our relationship began. The bathroom was across a hall and it all felt a bit squalid and reflective, I suppose, of the fact that no matter what, we were committing adultery. We hadn't meant to have an affair, but we were both so in need of someone to be with that it rapidly became one. I used him, and he used me, but we were consenting adults and he was a kind and caring soul.

Janet was delighted by what she thought was our friendship as it meant that he stopped turning up on her doorstep in states of abject misery and she could get on with arguing with Chris and her coterie, something which seemingly gave her great joy.

Sexually it was as it had been before for me with men, all right but not exciting. Pete was solicitous of my needs and over the course of six months or so I realised that he was growing ever fonder of me and wanted to occupy more and more of my time. Accepting that he and Janet were over, he moved to Chelmsford and bought a starter home, a small box of a place on an identikit estate. He was excited when I agreed to go there and meet his newly found friends.

We left his place and walked around the corner. Soon I was sitting squashed into a lounge room exactly like his, meeting some perfectly nice people who were not at all like me. After a few drinks, we piled into a taxi and went to a Chinese restaurant in the centre of the town. Pete was in good form, showing me off and hinting that I might move in soon. The prospect of living somewhere like that sent shafts of ice through my heart. I sat in the restaurant and felt a familiar emptiness.

Our relationship would have carried on for a while, I suppose, except for the fact that I managed to get pregnant. This was at the same time that he wanted to tell Janet about 'us'. I knew that he wanted kids and I knew that I had now trapped myself and had to do something. I also knew that it would be so easy to drift into having a child and moving in with him, but the overarching emptiness inside told me it would be the wrong decision.

One of the places that we processed samples for at UCH was the Marie Stopes Clinic, which was a few minutes' walk from work and one of the pre-eminent places for terminations of pregnancy. I made an appointment and sat with two other nervous women and joined them in filling in forms about our menstrual and sexual histories. In order to obtain an abortion two doctors had to confirm your sanity and suitability for the procedure. Sadly, the underlying attitude from the male medic who saw me was that I had been stupid to get pregnant. He told me none too pleasantly that he was quite within his rights to make me feel as badly as possible about deciding on a termination in order, so he said, to make sure that was what I wanted. I managed to wipe the smile from his face when I told him that I was on the Pill, and a high dose one at that. Put that in your pipe and smoke it, pal.

That night I sat at home wondering what to do. As a result of my lassitude in giving my life some direction, I had drifted into a situation that threatened to harm a lot of people, especially me. I had ultimately been advised by the doctor at the clinic that it was not a good idea to see the pregnancy through as having been on hormones there was the possibility of birth defects. Yet, I now found myself unable to face having the abortion.

I had told nobody and intended to keep it that way. I knew that I no longer wanted Pete in my life, but that didn't seem to alter the way I felt about his potential child. He had, I knew, told Janet that we were having an affair and she had not been pleased. I did question her sanity and her intention, but no more than my own. I felt like a rudderless fool. I spent most of that night, and the best part of a bottle of brandy, thinking about what a mess I was making of things.

Ultimately there was only one sane thing to do. I booked a termination for the following week, on a day when I knew that Jenny would be out for the evening. I was collecting secrets of my own now. It was a difficult week and the nearer the day came the more difficult it became. I had no idea if I would really go through with it.

Then, the day before I was to have the procedure I woke up with a pain that I recognised so well, a pain I'd had every month since I was thirteen.

I can't recall the exact excuse I gave Pete for ending our relationship. I do know that Janet bore the brunt of his apparent despair. Shortly afterwards she and Chris parted company, and Chris being in need of solace found Pete. Life is often something you couldn't make up, and some time later they married and had children together.

Over the next months I retreated further into myself. People were far too messy and took too much energy. The episode had been important, though, as I had come to the realisation that I had to be more honest about my own needs and desires and no longer a bystander in other people's lives.

I still felt at a loss, and although I did have a couple of good friends at UCH they had partners, and lives, of their own. I found life harsh and grey. The entertainer mode that I used at times of stress became harder to resurrect. Then when in need of people most, I fouled my patch with the other staff. This was in 1982, when the Falkland Islands were invaded by the British forces.

There was a research facility within the block that housed the routine laboratories. It had a small staff and one of them was Riccardo, who just happened to be Argentinean. He was a lovely chap, softly spoken and kind. One day in the coffee room I found him sitting at a table alone; the atmosphere around him was Antarctic. Nobody was speaking to him. Maggie Thatcher had just launched her campaign and Riccardo represented the enemy. I couldn't believe the stupidity of people.

In the East End, the antipathy towards Germany had been a feature of my childhood and something I'd accepted growing up as I had among bombsites. Tales of death during the Blitz and my experiences with Holocaust survivors made it difficult for me not to remain suspicious of that country.

This situation was very different, engineered as it was by a failing prime minister and a group of power-hungry generals fighting over a sheep-infested bunch of rocks of no great relevance to the world. When Riccardo left the coffee room I tried to discuss the situation with my peers, only to find that I rapidly became regarded as an 'Argie-lover'. It was crazy, and as the country descended into a jingoistic frenzy life became increasingly difficult for Riccardo and his countrymen.

He and I spent a lot of time together as befitted our newly awarded outsider status. He tolerated it all with a dignity I doubt I would have summoned, but then he was alone in a sea of born-again 'Rule Britannia' chanting numbskulls. Once we 'won' the war things calmed down and we reached an equilibrium of sorts, but it was never the same again.

The work itself continued to remain interesting, but I had been doing it for a good while and it was time for something new. The situations vacant in my field offered nothing exciting and at that point fate took a hand.

One afternoon a small woman wearing round horn-rimmed glasses wandered into the lab looking for me. She was Nancy Hogg who worked in the research laboratories in another part of the medical complex and was an expert in macrophage biology.

'I was told you did coagulation.'

She went on to explain that the solution that she was carrying on ice in a beaker was a monoclonal antibody that she had generated called UC45. She suspected that it interfered with coagulation, but she had no way of testing it. I was always busy during the day with the routine load, but I said I could stay behind after work and play with it.

'It's precious, I don't have much of it, so do you mind if I sit with you?'

I didn't usually like people looking over my shoulder but this was no doozy medic with a God syndrome. I asked around and found out that she was the world expert in her field. She had a transatlantic accent and during our discussions I discovered that she was Canadian and married to a geneticist called Mike Fried.

We spent many an evening working through a panoply of tests that we devised to see what the antibody interfered with. One evening she asked me if I'd considered doing full-time research. I'd already co-authored a few papers on various aspects of my field, so thought I had a fair idea of what that may entail.

'It seems to me you'd be missing a trick if you didn't give it a try.'

'What would I do then?'

'There's another world of science out there.'

She'd seen the hurry and the urgency of the routine laboratory. It was not a place she felt comfortable in; hers was a more stately, considered approach to science. I thought about it. Was I just drifting on the wind again or being presented with a real opportunity? Nancy offered me a space in her laboratory in which to study if I managed to get onto a recognised course. I decided to see if I could get a day release from work to study with her, which meant I could afford to live and maintain my lifestyle.

My qualification in medical laboratory sciences was not recognised as a degree, so I couldn't register for a PhD. I went and saw the head of the haematology research laboratories, Professor Ernie Huehns, for advice. He had escaped from Nazi Germany to England with his mother and was one of the leading experts in the field of thalassaemia. I was told that using a car battery, some wires and buffer solutions, he had established one of the cornerstones of the diagnostic tool of electrophoresis. I figured that he would have a good idea as to what I should do and what was possible.

He knew Nancy and was surprised that she had offered me a place. It transpired that I could register at UCL for a master's degree, but only if I sat the MRC Path written exam and passed. This was the degree that doctors took to become members of the Royal College of Pathologists. I was almost put off by this as it really was a difficult exam.

Ernie was a strange mixture of largesse and parsimony so one never knew quite what was coming next. 'I will pay for you, if you pass the MRC Path exam that is.'

'Will you pay for that too?'

'Yes.'

'And the study days with Nancy?'

'I'll smooth your path. But be aware the qualification will be an MPhil, but will really be a PhD.'

'Why?'

'That's just the way it is.'

Unfair as that was, he was as good as his word and paid for everything.

I wondered a few months later, when I hijacked the Queen Mother when she was visiting to open Ernie's new laboratories, if he'd change his mind about the rest. Some of we technical staff were recruited to make the new place look lived in while Her Maj was given the grand tour. I was studying avidly for the exam, so was engrossed in a book and some slides when I became aware of a pair of feet. I looked up and saw a badly hemmed purple velvet coat and almost fell off my stool into a curtsy. I remember thinking that Mum would have hemmed it so much better.

Ernie was staring at me and pointing to his watch. The Queen Mum was on her own time schedule and asked me what I did. I told her then delivered the fateful words.

'I imagine you know a bit about haemophilia, having it in the family?'

As soon as I'd said it I could see myself in the Tower of London.

She smiled. 'I don't bother myself with that side of our history.'

I thought Ernie was going to have an apoplectic fit as she then asked me what was down the microscope in front of me. She looked at the slide I had been studying and chatted some more. Her blue eyes twinkled with merriment. She thanked me and moved on to question somebody else.

Ernie grabbed me.

'Why did you say that?'

I'd just been reading about the Romanovs and haemophilia in the royal families of Europe.

'It's treason,' he said in his heavily accented English.

He looked over to where the Queen Mother now stood.

'Oh no!'

Rosemary Gale was one of the scientists in charge of developing new diagnostic techniques, one of which was using amniocentesis to detect if a foetus was homozygous for thalassaemia, in which case a termination was advised. It was reliable in approximately 75 per cent of cases. The technique was new and a sample had just arrived in the laboratory. The royal visitor peered over Rosemary's shoulder and was about to begin quizzing her when Rosemary turned.

'If you don't mind, ma'am, there's a woman on an operating table waiting to hear if she keeps her baby or not.'

'Oh, I see, so sorry my dear.'

With that the cavalcade moved on and the Queen Mum got into her limo and drove off. She would be home just in time for her legendary gin and tonic.

Chapter 16

The Early Eighties

At this point Rob decided to reappear. I was at work when he sauntered in with a set of six cheap crystal wine glasses as a present. Odd, the things you remember. Nevertheless, we met up a couple of nights later in a subterranean bar called The Warren, near to the station of the same name. I loved the place; it was all alcoves, candles, decent wine and no muzak with which you had to compete for conversation. It was as if nothing had happened, he was working in another lab and said he'd missed me.

'No ulterior motive then?'

He laughed and I noticed that his teeth were an unnatural shade of white. He was expensively dressed, even for him. He'd always been like a dog led by his tail, but his eyes were constantly sweeping the room looking for attractive men.

'I didn't come out for you to spend the night on the hunt. If you want me to stay, look at me.'

He was upbeat but gave nothing away except that he'd had some great holidays in New York and San Francisco.

It was the summer of 1982 and in London a man called Terrence Higgins had just died.

*

Looking back on it, HIV has been part of my life far longer than it has been of most people's. The arrival of the virus and its aftermath changed my life and the lives of those around me. It brought out the worst and the best in people, and galvanised the gay and lesbian communities like nothing else had ever done. For those of us working in the fields of haematology and blood transfusion it was a period of great uncertainty and often fear, as we had no idea what we were handling.

It's hard to recollect the exact dates, but some time in 1981 a man in his mid-thirties collapsed. He had brought his mother and his male lover to Europe from San Francisco for a vacation and I think his name was Simon. As it is for many people who were involved in the early days of AIDS, things are a bit of a blur. Simon was brought into UCH.

One of his first symptoms was bruising due to a low platelet count, so he ended up at my door. Within a short period of time his symptoms resembled that of aplastic anaemia, where the blood is bereft of white blood cells. In short, his immunity was compromised. He was handed over to the cancer team and had a bone marrow transplant, which failed. He also developed odd purple lesions, but before he could be further diagnosed, he passed away. I remember that his boyfriend had slept at the bottom of his bed on the floor throughout, and I can still recall his sobs when Simon died. I'd been about to take some bloods for more coagulation tests when he breathed his last. Some of his serum was stored in liquid nitrogen and several years later, when the penny dropped, we had it analysed. He had been HIV positive.

Reports had been coming in about the 'gay plague' which was then assaulting the USA. Then the received wisdom was that the syndrome was caused by an overexposure to seminal protein transferred during anal sex between men. Of course, this was scientific idiocy, but such was the pervasive, ramped-up homophobia by the Reagan administration that it was accepted as a logical reason. Gay men had to be the source of the disease, case closed.

From 1982 onwards reports of haemophiliacs having the same symptoms began to appear. I heard about a group that had recently formed called Gay Men's Health Crisis in New York who seemed to be the only people who were active in disseminating information. A man called Larry Kramer was spearheading the group. I wrote to him asking what their theories about the origin of AIDS were and seeking any advice they may have. A couple of weeks later a large bundle of papers arrived at work.

Paula Bolton-Maggs was a part-time registrar who was in effect given to me. She was slender, blonde, very religious, sang hymns under her breath, wore the most outrageous knee-length woolly striped socks, had two young children, a husband and was utterly dedicated to the patients.

Her favourite hummable tune of the moment was 'Onward Christian Soldiers', which she was now delivering sotto voce as I studied the documents. Several A3 sheets of paper were covered in diagrams of the most extreme sexual practices that took place between gay men and advising that people desist from indulging in them.

'I can't imagine that any of our haemophiliacs would indulge in such, can you?' she said, trying to figure which way up to hold a set of illustrations of arms or feet being inserted into anal orifices.

I shook my head. 'This is all a wild goose chase. It's got to be transmissible. It has to be an organism. This isn't protein overload.'

She agreed, and we held our breath waiting for whatever caused AIDS to be discovered.

Over the years I had been forced to buy cheaper coagulation factors. Our European supplier was deemed too expensive, so I had purchased the products from the USA. It was known that the prison population was the source of much of this, but as the bloods were tested for all known pathogens it seemed safe.

Of course, it transpired that needle sharing was one of the ways that HIV was transmitted from person to person, and so prisons provided the perfect incubator for the virus. That knowledge lay in the future, but for now we were on a knife edge as the deaths in the gay and haemophiliac communities mounted and nobody had a clue what was causing it.

From time to time I'd met up with Faye, who was now working in another London teaching hospital. She'd gotten over her SM club phase and was concentrating on a new hobby, photography, which kept her out of trouble. I wanted to see a film called *Another Way*, which was a story based on the life of two women in Hungary who meet and fall in love. It had won the Palme d'Or at Cannes and came highly recommended. She readily agreed to see it with me.

It has to be said, it is one of the most depressing films ever made and, like most evocations of lesbians even to this day, one of them dies. Shot in the snow; the red of communism bleeding into the white of love. The other is paralysed from the neck down.

It was in one of the alternative cinemas in the Brunswick Centre in Bloomsbury, a place which is all concrete and hard edges with few redeeming features. A bit like the life under communism we had just seen depicted.

'Well, that was a bundle of laughs,' Faye said, as we walked out into a classic London drizzle.

We went for a couple of drinks in a nearby pub to chew over the film, which although bleak had been powerful.

'Fancy being so suppressed,' she said.

I peered silently into my drink. I too was not a bundle of laughs.

'Come on Lin, lighten up.'

I was crumbling under the pressure of work and my fears for my patients, at least that was what I told myself. Had I been honest, the caution with which I increasingly approached life and which stopped me from finding out who I really was remained at the heart of my difficulties. The person I had become held herself at a distance from the world. It was seldom that I allowed my emotions to erupt to the surface; that way I calculated I could survive without losing myself.

My ability to feel through my skin meant that thunderstorms were exciting as the electricity in the air was

palpable. In day to day life I was similarly able to sense
other people's emotions, but it was something that I didn't
welcome. Sometimes it was so intense and raw that I had to
hide away. It happened with patients, it happened with my
family, it happened and it was happening more often. It was
one reason I had never been able to be honest with friends
like Janet or Faye, or Jenny. I was fearful that I would not
be able to cope with their reactions and therefore my own.
Or was it pure cowardice?

Faye reached out and took my hand.

'Come on, spill the beans.'

'Oh work, you know? This blessed infection or whatever
it is and my patients.'

'That's not all of it, is it?'

'A bit.'

'And the other bit?'

I said nothing, my usual routine when in doubt.

'Have you ever thought of a relationship with a woman?'

There it was, THE question. I took a long while to answer.

'Why? Have you?'

'I think you know that I have.'

I said nothing.

After a long pause, she said, 'How about it?'

I was stunned by her bravura, her seeming ease with the
situation.

'Nobody need ever know. And if we don't like it, no harm
done,' she continued.

'I don't know.'

'Oh yes you do.'

As we parted that night she pulled me into a darkened

alleyway and kissed me. I went into denial mode. She left it at that, saying I should call her once I'd had time to think.

One week passed, then another. In the end I decided that it was time to find out if my fascination with women was anything more than just a figment of my overactive imagination. I called her.

'I thought I'd never hear from you again,' she said and laughed.

I talked about anything but the offer she'd made. She became exasperated.

'Look, are we going to bullshit around or are we going to do this?'

I agreed to go over to her place one Sunday when Ron was on call.

I had a Honda 90 moped which I had bought in order to get used to driving in traffic. I had failed two driving tests as I was so nervous of other cars, and to me it seemed the perfect answer. I shook inside from the moment I agreed to see Faye until I pulled up outside of her terraced, three-bedroom house in an affluent part of west London. Ron had inherited the house – it was something they would never have been able to afford themselves.

I didn't want what happened to be a cold and clinical event, a mere 'finding out' which way my sexuality lay. Nor did I want to hurt her in any way. Faye, always so calm and direct, was shaking too. Of course she had been interested in women, and me. Of course she'd wanted to ask me many times about myself.

Making love to her was not difficult. She had been married for over twenty years and had never had an orgasm.

As I write this I still can't believe that it was so, but it was. For the first time that I could remember on that afternoon, in front of the fire in her lounge, I let my emotions drive me. I stopped thinking, I just was, and it was glorious.

Having been the repository of so many secrets over the years I found keeping my own very difficult. Faye had told me not to say a word about us to anybody. It was rather like one of the characters in the film we'd seen had been made to act, and it made me feel tarnished to lie. I told Jenny that Faye was teaching me photography, which is hilarious as it is one of the things I have never been any good at. If Jenny noticed anything about my behaviour, she never said. Having been around Rob for so long I was acutely aware of my double standard and I wondered at my lack of bravery.

However, just at that moment, it seemed as if the part-decriminalisation of homosexuality in 1967 had never happened. The hysteria surrounding AIDS meant that the streets had become hunting grounds in which the belligerent and ignorant would taunt and assault people who they thought might be gay. Ignorance meant that lesbians were seen as part of the HIV problem too. How exactly we were supposed to be spreading the infection was not known, but nevertheless we were regarded as high risk by the powers that be. As a consequence, there was a collective closing of closet doors. The Thatcher government fed the fear that was generated and fed off it. Shameful and irresponsible like Reagan, they added years of suffering to the lives of people because of their hatred of difference. It wasn't the most propitious of times to come out.

On the positive side, I began to understand Rob a lot more as increasingly sex became like a drug to me. I felt like a teenager discovering it for the first time, which in many respects I was, and because of this I thought I was in love.

I made hints about Faye and me living together which were ignored, until finally I suggested it.

Faye laughed. She had exactly what she wanted, a stable nice middle-class home with a husband and all the frills of being accepted by society, and me for sex.

I felt like a toy, but I was hooked. I hated the cloak and dagger aspect, but like a sleep walker kept going. I hardly saw my family. I'd have felt too ashamed to confront them, as Mum at least would have seen that something was different, something that I would not discuss. I saw Janet from time to time, she'd forgiven me about Pete. I still kept silent about my sexuality. It was all too much of a habit to break easily and it still would have opened floodgates that I didn't want to face.

In the end the cracks began to appear. I'd forgotten to tell Jenny that I would be out one night. She was on call as was Ron, so I went to Faye's. I could have lied when she called me at work the following morning, demanding to know where I had been. She'd been really worried.

'I was with Faye.'

'Oh, more photography?'

'No.'

That night I told her what was going on. Her rage was incandescent. Of course her major consideration was that people would find out and assume that she was 'like that'. I had the whole book of potential calamities thrown in my direction and as she stood and ranted a window began to open up within me; I suddenly felt lighter. I didn't have to take this any more. But there was a game to be played before I would be free.

That week, I agreed to meet with Faye and Jenny in Patisserie Valerie on Old Compton Street in Soho. The lightness inside me meant that I didn't care what was said. I was untouched by the opinions that were being voiced as I sat and listened to the two of them fight to preserve their lifestyles with little consideration for my feelings.

They decided that the affair could and would go on, but it had to be kept secret. Faye was determined to hang on to me, Jenny was equally determined that her reputation be upheld as a straight woman and seemingly she wanted to hang on to me as well. As they sat and plotted they had no idea that the labyrinth of associations that joined us were being snipped asunder by a large pair of imaginary scissors that I had conjured up in my mind.

I sat and sipped my cappuccino and drifted off into a reverie. It was a nice late-summer's day and the clouds floated elegantly across the sky. I was heading for a breakdown of sorts and I knew it. I also knew I would survive, and I knew what I had to do in order to do so. Secrets destroy you in the end, I'd seen that so often in the past, and I wanted no more of this particular one. But timing is all.

Being alone was something I had never really thought about, but with the disastrous and unfulfilled relationships that lay around me it seemed to be the only way forward. You discover a lot about yourself – about your strengths and your weaknesses – when you are in extremis, and I learned a lot that year. As I write this I wonder why I didn't just walk away, but I am not the person that I was then. The world was a very different place and, in truth, where would I have gone? I suppose Janet would have taken me in, but I doubted I could have handled her high-octane household. When I finally told her about myself she too was incensed and rightly so. I had sat on the edge of her life observing but not being fully her friend. You cannot commit to anything or anyone fully if you live a lie.

So I played along with the plan of action that had been devised for me. In many ways life became easier, and in fact Faye and Jenny actually got on a lot better than they had ever done. With me as a pawn between them their futures seemed secure and they suffered under the illusion that I would just go along with it all for as long as they both wished. Faye, with her newly found sexual freedom, began a relationship with a married man that she met at a conference. There was no understanding of the pain she was causing me when she told me about it. She seemed blissfully unaware, it was all just a game to her and she took great delight in describing him, even down to his Union Jack underpants.

I backed off, citing my MPhil as a reason for having no time to see her so often. I had, against my own expectations, passed the exam to take up my degree. I found my studies with Nancy at the Imperial Cancer Research Fund fascinating. I would go one day a week, having collected samples for analysis during my visits to the operating theatres at work. My thesis was to be on varicose vein disease, but it was much broader than that and encompassed aspects of atherosclerosis and cell signalling, then in its early phases.

I learned a range of new techniques in the field of immuno-histochemistry, which at the time I had no idea would form the basis of another career. I had briefly studied histology but had never worked in that field. This relatively new branch of that science used microns, thin sections of frozen human tissue, and reacted it with tagged antibodies to identify cells and/or markers of inflammation or disease. The resulting colour combinations this produced was frequently like a work of art.

At lunchtimes there was a lecture by a world leader in their speciality. I purposely arranged my day-release from UCH in order to be at these. I loved the discussions that we had and the people I was working with. The more I became involved, the less my difficulties in the rest of my life had an impact. I spent hours of my own time studying in the library and slowly found myself being able to take part in the repartee in the ICRF laboratory, which at first had terrified me. It was all at such a higher level than anything I had known. Nancy pushed me; she knew that I was capable of more, and so I was. By the time she asked me to present my work to her group I realised that I felt that I really belonged. I worked on her antibodies as she further developed them and for the first time my mind began to sing.

One of the laboratory aides at ICRF was a woman called Pat Pretty who lived on Columbia Road and who had worked with my mum in the rag trade. She had almost fainted when I walked into the washroom one day to get some ice for an experiment. We had tea together in the staff canteen and she quizzed me about the family and myself.

'You don't come back ever?'

I shook my head. Pat had bought her flat in a tower block called Sivill House and was watching the area change. As she chatted on merrily I could see the street in my mind's eye.

'How's the market?'

'That's doing well. Died off for a bit but they sell a lot of cut flowers these days, seems to keep it going.'

'Are the wood factories still there?'

She nodded. 'And the dust, remember?'

I nodded.

'Some of the shops are boarded up. Shame. Some odd types have moved in. Arty farty. There are enough of us left, for the moment.'

'Ginger Lil?'

'Oh yes, still spreading rumours. She's a lonely old thing, though.'

I smiled at the warmth and lack of judgment that Pat exuded and which had been part of my experience of life on the street. She asked me about my degree and my work there. She loved her job because there were so many inter-esting people around from all walks of life and all parts of the world.

When I told Mum about Pat I felt the frost of ages down the telephone wire as she feared I would ask her to go visit her, as Pat had indeed asked.

'Your father needs me,' was her response.

'He'd like to go back.'

'That's as maybe, but the answer is no. He's in no fit state as well you know.'

Dad's arthritis had worsened to the extent that he required a knee replacement. These were experimental at the time and why he was considered a fit guinea pig I have no idea, but he was. I don't know what the alternative may have been, but the replacement was not the answer.

The flat they had was nice, but on the first floor without a lift. He had become a virtual prisoner in his home. Of course he hoped the op would allow him to walk again; it didn't. After two disastrous operations, which ended in him developing gangrene, he had his leg amputated from above the knee. During the final op he had a stroke from which he recovered well, but that left him incontinent.

Mum, stoic that she was, refused any help. She washed, clothed and fed him. Lifted him into and out of bed, refused any adaptation to the flat and wore herself out completely. Dad was her project in every way, as Clara had been mine. The level of care that was required and which she gave Dad was over and above anything any sane mortal of her age would have taken on. I wanted to organise respite care, but she'd have none of it. In the end we organised a rota system, so that at least she could go out to the theatre from time to time while one of us sat with Dad. Trapped in a chair, his life over, unable even to be wheeled onto the street. It was a sad ending of a life.

Chapter 17

Carol

Back in my world in 1984 I was planning my future. My calculations told me that given the probable sale value of the Barnet house, with my half of the profit and the savings that I was making, I could buy a lease on a one-bedroom mansion flat in Bloomsbury. I'd always been partial to the idea of living there and being able to walk everywhere I wanted to go.

I hadn't told anybody about this. Keeping all of the documentation at work, I calculated that I needed to save for another six months. This was a secret I could keep and I was happy knowing that I would soon be free. Six months didn't seem such a big deal in the great panoply of things. I did think of going back to Bethnal Green, but didn't pursue the idea. I didn't feel that I could cope with going home, no matter how enticing the thought of being wrapped in the familiar was. Bloomsbury was anonymous, I knew nobody, but it was near the growing central London gay scene.

Work wasn't going so well at this point. I hadn't counted on people being jealous of my degree being paid for. Stupid perhaps, but I didn't have much space inside my head for such thoughts. I was constantly checked up on by the senior

NHS lab staff to see if I was actually at the ICRF. Nobody there ever got in before 10 a.m., so I followed suit. We all stayed late and often went for a drink or a bite after the day's work. This didn't go down well with the UCH staff to whom beginning the day's work after 9.30 was anathema. I tried to explain, but I met a brick wall.

The real problem was that the Middlesex and UCH hospitals were in the throes of an amalgamation of sorts. Recently a medic whose expertise was coagulation had been appointed at the Middlesex and he had his own technical staff; more importantly he had an equivalent of me to whom he was inordinately attached. Paula was still part time and I knew that she and her husband would move on elsewhere at some point and, although she was excellent, she didn't sit well with the medical hierarchy. She spoke her mind too well and too often. I loved her for that but it did her no good.

The bottom line was I was surplus to requirements, and a war of attrition began. More and more of the interesting work was shipped down to the Middlesex and I was left in limbo. My day-release days were poorly covered by staff, and I'd come in to find results not reported and samples missing. The writing was on the wall, but I battled on as I wanted the degree.

I was still on tap, though, to save their bacon when needed.

I had a junior covering for me while I helped prepare the Christmas party of 1984. I'd had a few drinks and was on the wrong side of sober when one of the consultants called me to his room. I perfumed the air liberally with alcohol fumes as he told me that there was a patient next door who had cut himself shaving three days prior and was still bleeding. It transpired the chap was in his sixties and was a quite well-known Jewish hairdresser. A clotting screen had been done and it was normal.

I groaned inwardly. Mature and Jewish and male meant several things, but one in particular, if I was unlucky.

'Blood count?' I asked.

'Normal.'

It wasn't a leukaemia or thrombocytopenia, I was told.

'You sober enough to sort this?'

'Probably not. Why not come watch me,' I said with some vitriol.

He did, but not until I'd seen the patient for myself. He had an unobtrusive nick on his chin from which blood was flowing unchecked. A bin full of bloodied gauze sat at his feet. I knew then that I was indeed unlucky.

Of all coagulation factors, the most difficult to analyse are for what are called the contact factors. In order to accurately assay these, blood has to be taken in the gentlest of fashions and the test has to be performed without the sample coming into contact with anything except specially coated plastic tubes. The reagents cost a fortune and don't always behave as they should. Often you have to repeat the tests several times.

I looked at the consultant. 'My thinking is Factor XI deficiency.'

Coagulation wasn't his field. I knew that, so the semi-blank look was expected.

'He's a male Ashkenazi Jew. Factor XI goes down during life and in that gender, especially in that ethnic group,' I continued.

'If it's not that?'

I thought of Mr Muktar, the man who had developed antibodies to his own Factor VIII for whom diagnosing had taken days not hours, and hoped that it was what I thought.

A couple of hours later I finished the assay. I had been right, but now we had to treat him. Luckily you need very little of the factor to function normally, and as I watched he was infused with frozen plasma. Very shortly the bleeding stopped and the terrified look left his eyes.

I went upstairs and had a large drink. It was an OK party, everyone was obliged to attend and appear to have fun. Somebody always had a shag somewhere, usually in the medical secretaries' room, and everyone pretended it hadn't happened. I was chatting to Rosemary Gale from Ernie Huehns lab when a woman shyly walked into the room. She looked around until one of the other senior lab staff went over and shook her hand. She was to begin work with us in the New Year.

As we were introduced I noted the piercing blue eyes and quiet smile, and I remember thinking, 'Here's trouble.'

The blue-eyed woman was called Carol. She was Australian and had come overland to London from Kathmandu, and it wasn't until February that she came to work with me. The rotation to my section was for a month at a time.

She seemed pretty savvy and had been lecturing at the university in Perth, had a degree, but had become bored and decided to come to London. Or at least that was the story I got in the first instance. During our chats in the coffee room and over the water baths, in which most of the testing was done, I learned that she had hooked up with a man called Greg on the trip. He had gone back to Australia and, after she'd seen some more of Europe, she planned to go and live with him and possibly marry if it worked out.

It was on my radar that she was someone I would like to know very much better. You'd have thought that my life was complex and difficult enough and it was, but as she was obviously straight, the idea of anything ever happening was just that, an idea.

We got into the habit of going to The Warren for a drink. I asked her about her life and her trip and told her as little about myself as I could get away with. The last thing I wanted was the truth being exposed until I was good and ready. I talked a bit about Rob, however, and she about a gay man whom she'd known since she had been a student at the age of nineteen. They'd shared a house at one point and she seemed to have a group of gay male friends with whom she'd mixed and who were the basis of her social life.

Carol was six months younger than me and we had similar tastes in books, art and theatre, and as we talked I found myself edging towards talking about the reality of my life. I hadn't even shared my relationship with Faye with Rob.

Rob and I carried on with our on-off friendship, which sometimes veered towards something more, but I never crossed that line. I knew of at least one woman he'd had sex with, but it certainly wasn't the time to take any experiment in life to that level, although I came very close on a couple of occasions.

Rob had had every STD on the books, including syphilis, which I'd diagnosed one night before we were to go to a show.

'I've got a rash,' he'd said, showing me his back.

'Syphilis, penicillin tomorrow.'

And we'd continued with our evening. In the carefree world of the 1970s, sex had never been easier and recovering from its consequences equally so.

His friends, however, were now sickening and dying of this latest assault. As usual he had his own take.

One evening in Pimlico I lay with my head in his lap. Neither of us doubted that he would eventually be diagnosed as AIDS positive, as it was known then. HIV wasn't coined until 1986. 'It's a virus, it must be, and it can be beaten,' he said.

I said nothing and after a long pause he added, 'I had Terry Higgins you know. Being a bar man at Heaven, most of London did.'

Heaven, the gay nightclub, had opened in 1979 and I had been there with Rob on several occasions.

'I've never got the promiscuity.'

'I know you haven't. You're still a bit of a prude.'

'Nothing wrong with that.'

'Not unless it means you don't live a life.'

'And I don't?'

'No you don't. You are scared. You always have been.'

A few months later he was on his way to earn a lot of money in a laboratory in Riyadh in Saudi Arabia, where he assured me in his first letter home that the men were available and very amenable.

In 1984, Luc Montagnier and his team at the Pasteur Institute in Paris identified the retrovirus which we now know as HIV, and in spring 1985 Bill Dumbelton took his wife, Linda, on a cruise to celebrate his forty-second birthday. I had come to know Linda almost as well as Bill. Beneath the youthful, love-struck woman I had met those years before was a bright, sparky human being who knew which way was up and loved Bill with a fierce pride both of him and his accomplishments.

Before going on holiday, they had both been bled for a diagnostic test for the virus, which was fast tracked for those at risk. Of course, Bill wasn't the only patient of mine involved, but I had known him the longest and most intensely and in those eight years we had become good friends. We would kiss and hug on meeting, and after his marriage he always said that there were two Lindas in his life. I had seen him through the bleeds to his joints which had him crying with agony and an array of other more minor events which served to make his life difficult.

I can still see Bill's ashen face after he was told that he was HIV positive. The only glimmer of light was that Linda was negative.

He was not the only one of my patients to have the virus. As each of them were given their results, I felt that I had personally dealt them a death sentence.

People say, how could I have known? But that makes no difference; even to this day I look back with regret that I didn't fight for a cleaner source of blood for them all. It is true, how could I have known? But it affected me profoundly and pushed me into an almost manic state. I should have had counselling. I didn't. None was offered to staff or to HIV positive patients until very much later during the epidemic.

It was Tuesday, 16 April 1985, and I had agreed to go to the theatre with Carol. She was lonely and finding London difficult to crack, and as a Londoner she rightly figured that I knew my way around. It can only have been within a few days of my finding out Bill's status that I drove my moped over to the flat she shared with a couple of other Aussies in Hampstead. She was then a smoker and stood at the cooker with smoke curling into the air as she made a Stilton quiche. The flat was large and the lounge room had beautiful bowed windows overlooking a garden. The house itself was Georgian, and was chopped up into a range of flats which the landlord, a Mr Fisher, only let out to travelling Antipodeans. It was a lovely evening and very warm for the time of year.

The play that she had booked for us to see was *Gertrude and Alice* at the Hampstead Theatre. The story of the love affair between Gertrude Stein and Alice B. Toklas. Afterwards, we walked back to her place to finish off the sparkling Vouvray I'd brought with me. As we sat chatting, she was nervous, I gritted my teeth. Faye was being a real pain, wanting to see me more often. Jenny was in one of her extreme doldrums and wanted me at home. Life was not grand on any front, and I didn't want any further complexities to make it worse. The play had signalled what I thought was coming.

'Tell me about you and women,' Carol said.

'Why?' I almost spat out. 'Do you want me to make love to you like all the other nice straight women looking for a thrill?'

A bit of a drama queen statement, but that was how I felt.

She stared at me for a long time. I found that I was crying with anger and pain and sorrow for what I had come to see was years of wasted fear and emotion.

'I can't say no,' she said. 'I can't say no.'

'You may want to,' I replied. 'I have a very complicated life.'

She wanted me to tell her, and so I did. I figured that at any time she would be going back to Australia and I would never see her again. I needed to talk to somebody and she was it. When I got to the end of it she stubbed her cigarette out.

'You know they do say the best way to get over a love affair is to have another.'

I couldn't believe that she was real. Her nervousness had disappeared; she was all steely determination.

'And Greg?' I asked.

'Well, I am twelve thousand miles away.'

'And us working together?'

'If it works out I'll get a job elsewhere.'

'So simple.'

'Life can be.'

'But you are straight.'

'At the moment,' she laughed.

She sat and told me that her life in Perth had become untenable because, like me, she didn't know who she was. She had fallen in love with her gay college friend, but despite his preference for men she and he had been sexual partners on and off. Fortunately that aspect of their relationship had faded before he had contracted AIDS, with which he had been diagnosed before she left Australia to travel.

'I had affairs with married men, gay men and I fancied straight women.'

'Meaning?'

'I don't do commitment, I suppose. I came to London to find out who I am. It would have been so convenient for all my gay friends if I too was gay, so I came a long way away to find out for myself. Somewhere where nobody knows me and nobody can pressurise me into doing what I don't want to.'

I asked her how she really felt about Greg, who sounded like a nice stable man; she said she wasn't sure. Like me with Pete, it had seemed like a good idea at the time, but there was no grand passion involved. Greg had been nice and warm to cuddle in the deserts of Baluchistan and it had been great to have a male travelling companion in some of the far-flung corners of the world she had visited.

She told me she had tried sex with women who were gay and it had not been a good experience or, as she put it, 'Not for me.'

I asked why she wanted another try.

'With them it was a technical exercise, I wasn't attracted to them.'

'And me?'

'That's different.'

It was. She doesn't remember our first meeting at the party, but I can see it as clearly as if it were yesterday. More lust than love at first sight perhaps, but there had been something different for me from the very beginning. For the first time I found that I could be open and honest and completely myself. Our relationship began a short while later but not before I told Faye that it was curtains for us. She naturally thought me having two women in my life was fine, after all she was still indulging in her sexual voyages. I demurred, I had no desire to have a string of people sucking my emotional lifeblood, as I saw it. More than that, although my parents' marriage may not have been one of grand passion, it was what I knew and what I had observed and it had worked. I have never understood the concept of bed-hopping for kicks. Knowing who I was had turned out to be difficult enough without having multiple partners to tell me what I was and moreover what they needed.

I woke up on the morning that Carol and I had spent our first night together, which was in my home in Barnet to the sound of Pink Floyd's *The Wall* reverberating through the house. It was five in the morning and the smell of frying bacon filled the air. We sat on my single bed and ate bacon sandwiches and talked.

Her attitudes were so positive, so different from those of anyone else I had ever known. She brought with her a sense that anything was possible and a hint of the wide-open spaces from which she came. I told her that I wanted out of the house, and possibly my job. I was logical enough to think that I could use Carol as a lever to free myself from some of my past. It was too early to discuss what I saw as the inevitability that she would be returning to Australia, or even whether what we had just shared may develop into something more than just a good time.

True to her tenet that anything was possible, within three weeks she'd taken another flat in the house in Hampstead as sole tenant. It wasn't luxury, but it was a delicious time of freedom for us both. I shed my skin of fear and relaxed for the first time possibly ever. She was open, honest and fun, and saw absolutely nothing wrong in our relationship, or with me. She did find being in the closet at work difficult, but other than that life was a revelation.

Carol freely admitted that it was I who was taking the chances as London was my home town. She, on the other hand, could high tail it home and nobody need ever be the wiser. Of course she wasn't fool enough not to realise that coming out was not something you did lightly. As a friend of ours later put it of a well-known lesbian actress, who had seemingly rediscovered her hetero credentials when she landed a job in the USA, 'You can't put toothpaste back into the tube.'

I had the house in Barnet, and given that the accommodation Carol now had was on a par with my Tottenham flat I'd had those many years ago, it may have seemed obvious that she should move into the house, but that I could not countenance. Carol meant liberation, and the house meant more arguments and pain. I wasn't absent all of the time, but pretty much, and on those nights that for whatever reason I was home, Jenny would try and talk me into not leaving. Conversations went on into the early hours of the morning. It was exhausting and I just wanted out. On one of those final nights, just after I had told her that I wanted my half of the sale price of the house, she suggested that she may allow me the very thing that I had wanted for so many years, a physical relationship, if I stayed.

It could have been a heartbreaking instant, but I just felt angry and used. If ever a moment had been misjudged, that was it.

Had she really cared for me all of those years, but been unable to face the reality of it? I have no idea. All I know is that, some quarter of a century later, when we met at a mutual friend's engagement party, she cut me dead.

Despite my best attempts otherwise, Faye continued to contact me and finally Carol and I met with her in a restaurant in the West End. Halfway through the evening I went and hid in the toilet for a good fifteen minutes. I had a streaming cold, a headache and had had enough of her. When I emerged, Faye was still in full flood telling Carol that she would ruin my life and should just be a good girl and go back to Australia. Carol, on the other hand, was perusing the wine list; as I approached she smiled up at me. Faye was history.

Carol wasn't mentioning going home and I wasn't mentioning any permanence in a joint future. I was just so happy to coast along. It was a lovely spring and summer, but not without its challenges.

Six weeks after we had begun our relationship in earnest, her parents were to visit from Perth. The morning that they arrived I had to push her out of the door to go to the airport. At first she had wanted to tell them about me when they landed. I didn't think that after over twenty-four hours of travel they would need anything else other than a shower, meal and a sleep. For her, the reality of our relationship was interceding on her idyll in London. Until then she had been acting out her new life thousands of miles away from home, incognito as it were. The arrival of her parents signalled a step change in that. I washed up, vacuumed the flat and prepared to return to my house for a while, with all that would entail.

I met her folks the next evening after work. Her father, a tall, rangy man, had an easy laugh. Her mother was pleasant enough but less at ease with herself. They were to be over for a few months and the first trip they took was with Carol when they visited Ireland. It rained non-stop apparently and the only real view of the sights was on postcards.

After they came back, one night I slept in the flat, the excuse being that I'd had a few too many drinks to drive home. Possibly true, but mostly not. Early the next morning Val, her mum, found us lying in one another's arms on the spare mattress on the floor in the front room. The cat was out of the bag and Val said she'd never sleep again. Carol was bemused. Val had enjoyed the company of Carol's coterie of gay male friends and she found the response hard to handle.

'It's different when it's your own,' I said, as we sat in The Warren.

'I don't see why.'

'We're outside the society they know and understand, aren't we?'

To give her parents their due I was invited back for dinner that evening, and although not easy with the situation they were kind and friendly. A couple of nights later, Reg, her father, asked me out on my own. We wandered into a pub nearby. I knew that he hated London and the restrictions on space, the smallness of it all. It was like an alien planet to him. He sat with as cold a lager as the pub could summon up.

'I don't have nothing against you girlie, but save yourself

the trouble. Carol never lasts any more than six months with anybody.'

'You warning me off?'

'No, it's the truth. Though you'd be better looking than my other son-in-law.'

I almost screamed at the back-handed compliment, but didn't. He didn't have the vocabulary, and why should he? He'd been a car mechanic in a small country town south of Perth for most of his career. I was possibly the most exotic thing he'd ever met. Despite this we passed a pleasant enough evening together and I sensed that if I made his girl happy, he wouldn't mind a bit.

I hadn't been home to Bethnal Green for over five years when one night I was persuaded to take Reg, Carol and a friend, David, who she'd met on the overland trip, to savour the delicacy that was eels and mash. Her mum declined to come. I took them down Broadway Market to the place I had so often gone with my grandmother.

I had mentioned to Carol that I came from the East End but had not elaborated on it. Ghosts don't bother me and I was glad to feel Isabella's presence, if only imagined, as I taught them how to roll the eel around your tongue to liberate the bone. I wondered, if she appeared, what they would have made of her, and vice versa. I doubt it would have fazed her. I caught a whiff of orris root as we left, my mind was playing tricks. As we walked back I almost took them on a detour via Columbia Road, but I wasn't ready.

*

'They keep asking me what I am going to tell Greg,' Carol said, as the parents' trip neared its end.

'Nothing I'd say, you don't have a schedule.'

'No.'

I knew that she and Greg wrote to one another regularly, and it was only a matter of time before the pull of conformity would kick in. What we had was special, fun and rather wonderful, but I had no doubt that she would be going home. A few weeks later, after her parents had left and I was thinking of beginning to view flats, she dropped the bombshell. Greg had written to say that he was coming over at Christmas to take her home.

'I got the letter a couple of weeks back.'

'Oh?'

'I had to have time to think.'

I was about to say all of the comforting things I had rehearsed, about how it had been fun and how I was happy with her leaving, but my throat had closed up.

'I've just written back.'

We had one of those pauses that go on forever; I could see that she wasn't sure if she should tell me.

'I'm staying.'

'You what?'

'I told him all about us. I am not going home, Lin. I'd be crazy to. I've found what I've wanted, why would I give up on that?'

'But you have to.'

'Why?'

There was no real why, I'd just thought that for once I had a plan that might work. I wasn't sure if I could handle any more of the merry-go-round. Buying a flat in the centre of town had seemed like the ideal opportunity for me to have a level of independence that I had never had. I told her I wasn't sure that I could take on any more emotional trauma. She was Australian, what were we to do about that if we stayed together. She was too old to get a long-term visa and I was in a similar position with Australia. A long-distance relationship of thousands of miles did not appeal.

She laughed. 'I have UK grandparents, I can stay as long as I like. Don't you want me to stay?'

Of course I did.

Her great positive attitude took a real denting when she wrote home and told her friends about me. Assuming everyone would be happy for her, the bile, vitriol and frank stupidity that some people wrote made her weep.

'How can I be a threat to her children and everything she believes in?' she asked of a girlfriend she had travelled the world with some years before. People she'd felt she could trust showed their homophobic colours, others she might have thought would react badly were fine. I had exactly the same experience; it was odd who remained as friends.

As her qualifications were not accepted by the Medical Laboratory Sciences Institute as worthy of a senior position, Carol secured a job in research at Watford General Hospital. It meant driving the old Nissan car that her dad had bought up the M1 every day, but she did it. It wasn't exciting, but it paid the bills and led to a new career.

Chapter 18

Return to Columbia Road

As Christmas neared, Carol heard that two of her best friends, Les and Ray, a gay couple, were coming to London. She offered them the mattress on the floor. Their visit was important to her. For the first time she felt that she was meeting them on her own terms, not theirs.

We had a great time showing them London, they were excellent company. Some nights they'd go off to the bars alone, other times we'd go with them. One notable evening Les had found out about a bar in Dean Street, Soho. We arrived about midnight and as we descended the stairs into the smoke and murk the first thing we saw was an ancient bald and toothless man wearing just a nappy with a very large safety pin in it. There was an entrance fee for non-regulars and we certainly were that. The bar lady was a seven-foot-tall black man in a white leotard dress and the clientele a mix of ladies of the night and people of all sexual persuasions. I had a sense that gay life in Perth wasn't quite so colourful.

Christmas Day approached and Les desired a tree. They were staying into the New Year and wanted to celebrate everything in what they saw as a traditional fashion.

'I've found out about this neat market where we can get one,' Les said, as we sat over breakfast. It was Saturday, 21 December 1985.

'Where?' asked Carol.

'A place called Columbia Road.'

The room dissolved around me. I was aware of figures seated around a table and I was one of them, but I wasn't there. Two simple words and I was gone, back onto the street. The flat was not a place for quiet solitude, so somehow I negotiated a trip to the shops to buy something irrelevant. There was a churchyard nearby and I sat on a frost-laden bench within it and tried to understand why my heart was pounding.

Columbia Road, the sound of sawmills, the stench of Clara's accidents, Mum's laughter, Nan sucking the life from a piece of toast; and that last time she had spoken to me, her words singed into my memory.

'There's a bit of you that will always be here, even when you don't know it. It'll sneak up on you one day.'

It was a childish recollection I knew, but one which made me ache wholeheartedly. I wanted a world which no longer existed.

Over the past month or so, Carol and I had been talking about moving in together and buying our own place. We'd had a look at a few flats in Kentish Town, all ghastly. I'd never mentioned Columbia Road, not a word. Once my parents had left I had excised any thought of the street as acutely and cleanly as a scalpel removes a boil. But it had taken just two words to reverse that. With my mind dancing with memories I brushed the frost from my clothes and headed to the flat. When I got back Les and Carol were poring over an *A to Z*.

'So how do we get there?' Carol asked Les.

'I know the way,' I managed to say.

The next day was cold, clear and crisp as Carol drove down from north London into the labyrinthine streets that I knew so well. We parked on Hackney Road and walked down Horatio Street, through Ezra Courtyard and into the street. All three of them were excited; the market was in full flood and packed. I'd never seen it so vibrant. Most of the shops it seemed were dedicated to the sale of pots and goods to support and complement the market.

As we walked past my old house, I looked up at the window out of which Clara had stared those many years ago. I didn't have to close my eyes to visualise her. The street hadn't changed, why would it? Beneath the ebullience of the market it was its own wonderfully shabby, quietly jaded self. Even though the factories didn't mill on Sundays, I was sure that I could detect the waft of wood dust dancing in the air.

Loaded up with decorations and with a tree purchased, Les marched us into the Royal Oak. We hassled good naturedly for four chairs and soon sat with drinks in front of us. I wasn't seeing the bar as it was, but as when my grandmother Alice had sat downing pints with her cronies. When Diamond Lil belted out her numbers.

'A real East End experience,' Les said, as we were given some seafood to eat.

We laughed at his complete bewilderment as he picked up a whelk.

'Disgusting,' he said, manfully trying to chew the unchewable.

'An acquired taste,' I said with difficulty.

Carol noticed. 'Is there anything wrong?'

I knew that I had tears in my eyes. 'Nothing, absolutely nothing.' I took a deep breath. 'I have to come home, that's all.'

'Home?'

'Two doors away. I lived there for the first twenty-three years of my life.'

She looked at me with frank incomprehension.

'You never said you came from here when Les mentioned this place.'

'I left a while ago.'

'And now you want to come back, just like that?'

'Yes. It seems so.'

There was one of those silences that hang off a precipice, but being the adults that we were we managed to bypass a fall. We got on with our day, but when we were finally alone that evening she wanted to know what was going on.

Even then I couldn't be honest with her. I talked about the fact that we could buy a house there for what a flat would cost anywhere else. It was central, easy to get to places from. I was all logic. My emotions told me otherwise.

'But it's still rough and dangerous.'

My fear was that she would say no. In those few hours since our visit I had realised that all of my life I had been looking for someone who I could take home with me;

someone who would understand the lyricism that I found in that grotty street as something real and not a cause for laughter. With whom I could share the memories that were so difficult but so important. Carol's view of the East End naturally was that of most outsiders. Dickens still defined the area, and to her it was not a place she wanted to be.

'I'm a bit flummoxed,' she said.

I didn't tell her until much later of a feeling so powerful and overwhelming that there was no debating my decision. Carol took some persuading, not least because she was convinced that we'd have problems because of our sexuality.

I told her not to worry about that, and on a sunny January day we viewed a house on the Jesus Hospital Estate, a Victorian cottage which overlooked a green. The sun was streaming through the front room window and although it needed work, we liked it.

Mr Verlander had owned the house for two years and he liked both it and the area. His wife, however, wanted to move even though she had a mere five-minute walk to work.

'I love it, she hates it.'

I asked him why.

'She can't see what lies beneath,' he said without any irony.

Carol and I exchanged a glance.

'She only sees the grot,' he continued.

He loved the raw edginess and the history. He showed us maps of the area that he'd collected and waxed lyrical in a way I had never heard from an outsider.

Afterwards we walked along the Regent's Canal nearby. It was not the loveliest of places for a discussion and Carol kindly ignored the scum and the detritus that floated on the water's surface.

'Why come back?' she asked.

'I have to.'

'You must tell me, Lin.'

I talked about the wood dust, Diamond Lil and Maisie, the people I knew, painting the scenes as best I could. I didn't make too good a job of it. The one person I didn't mention was Clara.

'That's in the past. Your childhood.'

'I know.'

'Well?'

She stared at me for a long time, knowing that wasn't the full story.

'All right, if it means that much to you.'

There was still so much I wasn't telling her and my logical mind knew that returning to the area was not necessarily a good idea. However, my skin was calm, which meant something I supposed.

We put an offer in and began the five-month journey to buying the house. My brother, who came to look at it with me, was confused. We too sat in the Royal Oak after we'd prodded and poked around the kitchen and taken up some floorboards.

'You're barmy, these houses are as damp as hell, you know that.'

'I want to come home.'

'Why, for crying out loud. You'll lose your money.'

'I am going to do this.'

'Mum won't be happy.'

'Mum's not buying it.'

Mum indeed was not happy, as expected given her now very developed antipathy to the area.

'It's my life.'

'Up to you,' she spat out and went into the kitchen of her flat and played a samba with the pots and pans.

Dad smiled at me broadly as she left the room.

'You can come visit,' I said softly. 'We can carry your chair down the stairs.'

'I'd like that.'

Jenny said, or rather shouted, 'You should never have left the East End.'

'I never really did, did I?'

She gave me one last withering look as I left Barnet for the last time.

* * *

It is 17 May 1986, one year and one month and one day since Carol and I had our first date. The sun has been up for a while when she wakes to find me sitting on the carpet beside the bed.

'You haven't slept?'

'No.'

She waits, she is good at waiting, I have learned this during these past months when at any time I had expected her to decide to pull out of the agreement to move to Bethnal Green. During the long night I spent voyaging through my memories I have realised that there is much to say, much to share, but is now the time? She has committed so fully to me and my needs that to overburden this bright new day with the weight of my past seems selfish. She knows enough and we have our own journey to embark upon.

She tugs my ear. 'Out with it, Wilkinson.'

'Later.'

'Remember, no pauses, no lies, no avoiding the subject.'

This is what I have demanded of our relationship, given the obfuscations of my past. I take a deep breath and wonder what lies in wait for me on the other side of my tale.

'I need to tell you about Clara,' I say.

And I do, unlocking the final part of my heart that I have kept protected and hidden for so many years. I tell her it all, painting the scenes as I remember them in awful, yet glorious, technicolour. Carol lay on the bed in silence as the story wove towards its climax.

I tell her about the day I came home from primary school to see an ambulance standing outside our home, its back doors open. As I approached two men came out of the house, with Clara balanced uncomfortably on their shoulders. She was whimpering softly. I called her name, she turned and as she did a stream of urine ran down the back of one of their shirts, amber on white. An unruly rivulet of terror that meandered ever more slowly as the stain spread outwards.

I ran towards her, but they had obviously been warned that I might be trouble, and by the time I reached them she was sealed firmly in the back. I was almost eleven years old and she was gone.

Tears ran freely down my face at the memory. I had never forgotten how close Clara and I had been and how much I had wanted and tried to help her, but the acuteness of the memory surprised even me.

I could still hear Mum saying to me moments after the vehicle had driven off, 'You tried, Lin, let it go.'

'But . . .'

'All the buts in the world won't change the fact that we can't help her. Alice is old and she was only going to get worse. She had to go away.'

I hold Carol's hand. 'I felt like a traitor.'

And I had felt exactly that. I was forbidden from seeing her, but occasionally one of my aunts would visit and their reports back were whispered to Dad, who never had the courage to go. He justified his lack of visits by declaring that it was 'women's work'.

She was in St Matthew's Hospital on Shepherdess Walk near Old Street. It was an old workhouse and by the time she was there it held over 300 patients. Every time Mum and I went to Chapel Market in Islington we passed it on the bus, but we never went in. That part of our lives was closed I was told. I replayed the scene in my mind: the looming presence of the place on the corner of City Road was as thunderous a presence to me as the lorries which sped past its doors.

I did manage to see her once more. I'd caught a snatch of conversation between the adults about Clara being more unwell than usual, and I decided to try and visit. By age thirteen I was a large, bespectacled young woman who could pass for much older than her years. I remember the tall metal gates and the dim lighting which barely illuminated the place, but I don't recall the walk to the ward. I do recall the doors swinging open to reveal beds packed tightly together and a stench of bodily fluids that was ingrained into the fabric of the place. The noise was overwhelming and the scene like one from a Dickensian novel, as women in all stages of mental anguish and dementia cried, screamed and moaned. Some were tied to their beds; it was terrifying.

Clara's eyes had sparked when she saw me; she'd even managed the beginning of my name. All those years since we had seen one another and she still knew my name.

I had some photographs of new and old members of the family; I talked and talked, told her about them, what they were up to. Her eyes filled with tears as she cuddled the images to her chest. She was still in there. The acres of loss that I could see in her eyes was unbearable. I wanted to spirit her away in a taxi; to what?

I left the photos with her; she was staring at them as I left. I have never been able to wipe that image from my mind.

Carol held me until my tears had stilled and I could breathe normally.

'You do know that you could not have done any more?'

I did, of course, but the hurt was still there.

The next day was a Sunday and the lorries arrived at dawn. By 7 a.m. all the pitches on Columbia Road were full to bursting with blooms and plants of all descriptions and by eight the street was packed with people.

We wandered through it; some of the costermongers nodded to me as if I had never been away. The hope brought with spring infused us and, no matter that the house was bare of just about everything, we came home carrying armfuls of plants and bunches of flowers.

The street had put on its best show for us, but it was not this Columbia Road that I had come back for. It was for the quiet days when the street was bereft of all but those who lived here, or who knew it so well that it was on their daily route.

During the week it remained a frontier place where the odd and eccentric could find a home, a community. During those first weeks back I saw them, the young, the adventurous, enjoying their own very individual lives, embracing the difference of living here rather than elsewhere. Welcoming, accepting and curious, that is the street that was the backdrop to my life.

Over thirty years have passed since that day and still the ghosts of the past live on in parallel with the present, they always will. Diamond Lil may no longer hold court, Nan no longer sits supping her tea from a saucer and even the dust from the sawmills is no more. And Clara? What of her? She whose ghost rested so heavily within my heart for so long? As the years have passed and I remain, I have come to understand that she would have forgiven me for all that I could not do.

Epilogue

In 1986 I was still working at UCH, but by the autumn the combined pressures of the politics of the institution and the lack of support for me in dealing with the patients who were HIV positive led me to leave.

I continued to study with Nancy and got my MPhil, and as a consequence was offered a position as manager and research scientist at UCL's Rheumatology Research Unit, a job I adored. Research was my metier and working with Professor Jo Edwards and team was fulfilling both professionally and emotionally.

Since the late 1990s I have been writing full time. I left science for a variety of reasons, one being that I had always wanted to write. After years of proclaiming this, Carol told me to 'Put up or shut up', so I did the former.

This work ended on the note of ghosts and since I came home I have a few more to add to my list. Rob died of HIV, no great surprise there, but I miss his lunacy. Bill Dumbelton too died, not of HIV, but the stigma of being positive sullied his final years.

Carol and I became involved in the fight for equality and were the first women to sign the Greater London Authority's Partnership Register, paving the way towards gay marriage. My activism led to me becoming Chair of Amnesty International UK.

We still live in our house in Bethnal Green. The East End has changed enormously. My father had been right with his prediction that the area would be discovered. Yet, although change is inevitable, somehow Columbia Road, for all of its international fame, remains resolutely itself.

Acknowledgments

Firstly, I'd like to thank Hannah MacDonald of September Publishing for the skill, warmth and encouragement she has shared with me during the writing of this memoir. To my editor, Charlotte Cole, a salute for being incredibly precise and thoughtful throughout.

To all of the people who appear in these pages, you have ensured that my life hasn't been dull.

Linda Dumbelton for contacting me after many years and rekindling my memories of Bill and allowing me to share them.

Carol who has been endlessly patient and supportive throughout, and finally my family, which is small but perfectly formed. Thank you.